The Marriage Recipe

Recipe

A Guidebook for Wives—Biblical
Principles to a Better Marriage

MFON B. NWABUOKU

authorHOUSE®

AuthorHouse™
1663 Liberty Drive
Bloomington, IN 47403
www.authorhouse.com
Phone: 1 (800) 839-8640

Published by AuthorHouse 10/29/2018

ISBN: 978-1-5462-6136-0 (sc)
ISBN: 978-1-5462-6134-6 (hc)
ISBN: 978-1-5462-6135-3 (e)

Library of Congress Control Number: 2018911935

Print information available on the last page.

Osita and I dedicate this book to

Kenechukwu Nwabuoku- our priceless gift from God!

*You add a myriad of blessings too numerous to count
to our lives- you truly make us RICH!*

Contents

Acknowledgements

My heartfelt thanks to everyone whose support has been invaluable!

God- the Author and Finisher of my life: Everything I am and everything I have comes from You. I would be nothing and can accomplish nothing without You!

My husband-Osita: You are proof that God truly loves me! Every good memory I have, has you interwoven in it. I look into your eyes and believe I can do anything. Thank you for your endless love and support!

My son-Kenechukwu: I will forever praise God for the treasure that you are. My unequaled jewel, I look forward to all God has made you! Thank you for your love and support!

Pastor Ose Imiemohon: Thank you for taking the time to read my manuscript and for the feedback. And most importantly, thank you for always teaching me to believe in myself!

Pastor Lawrence Ladokun: I'll always credit you with kicking me into action! Your lessons on personal management and life course setting remain principles I work with. Thank you for always encouraging me to do more and be more!

Liz Heaney: You are a gift from God! Thank you for showing me how to turn my ideas into words that truly express the message I wanted.

Funmi Obabire: In the time I've known you, I've found a true friend and sister. Thank you for all your encouragement and support!

Foreword

When Mfon and I decided to get married, we agreed that no matter what might come, the constants in our marriage would remain God and our love for each other.

We have kept to that promise by applying God's principles to our marriage and that has helped to bring out the best in us and has made our marriage something we're both happy about.

The ingredients mentioned in this book are the same ones Mfon and I have used in our marriage over the last fifteen years and are based on the Word of God.

I am sure that this book will bless the reader- whether you are married or are planning to be.

Osita Nwabuoku

Introduction

Anyone Can Have a Successful Marriage

Marriage is a God-designed, intimate, and complementary union between a man and a woman in which the two become one physically. But it's not just any sort of union; it is a covenant--a sacred covenant.

What is God's purpose- His desire for this union? Why did God introduce marriage in the first place?

Marriage was created primarily for companionship:

Then the Lord God said, "I see that it is not good for the man to be <u>alone</u>. I will make the <u>companion</u> he needs, one just right for him." Genesis 2:18 (ERV)

Checking up on the meaning of those two underlined words, here's what I found-

To be alone is to be *"without others' help or participation: single handed"*[1]

And for the word 'companion', one definition struck me-

'Each of a pair of things intended to complement or match each other'[2]

So, here's the key thought here, marriage was intended to provide 'help'. It was intended to make life's assignment easier to fulfill. Here's the picture- let's say I was given the task of cutting down 100 trees, it would take me

less time and effort to do so if I had someone helping me and it would be more enjoyable too.

That's why God gave Adam a wife. Not because Adam could not fulfill purpose without Eve- he was doing so before she came along- but because with Eve by his side helping, he could achieve much more and better enjoy the journey.

In marriage I find a partner to complement me; one to match me, one to help me. In marriage I find a mutually beneficial relationship.

Not to be taken lightly, marriage is a man and woman taking an oath publicly before God (with God as witness and upholder) to be to each other all God desires them to be as man and wife.

I remember how excited I was as I was getting ready to take those vows. Even back then, I knew marriage was a big deal: I would be choosing one man to spend the rest of my life with. I wanted to be prepared for the journey, so I took our premarital classes seriously.

One statement from the seminarian who taught those classes has stuck with me through the years. He told us that marriage could either be "a prison or a paradise". Using my imagination, I envisioned what each of those kinds of marriages would look like for me.

For me, a marriage prison would be a place where:

🍴 **I feel lonely and unloved, as if I don't matter to the one I love the most.**

> Even though I have the physical presence of my husband, I feel as if I were alone and on my own. My pain, fears, dreams are important only to me, and even if I do share them with my husband, they fall on deaf ears, unacknowledged. Rarely, if ever, does my husband show me affection through a hug, a kiss, or kind words. I don't experience romantic moments except for those I read in magazines or observe in other couples.

¶ I feel hopeless, stuck.

Gone are all my childhood dreams of a happy home. I am bitter, disillusioned, and cynical, and believe that happy couples are a myth. If I see a couple that appears happy, I tell myself they are simply putting up a façade and are just as miserable as I am.

Angry because I feel powerless to change and blaming myself for my misery, I do hurtful things to myself: eating my way up the weight scale or constantly criticizing the way I look (I would want to be taller, slimmer, have more cleavage or a different nose). My self-image is so poor that I want to be every other woman but myself. I hear innuendos where none exist, see conspiracies in every relationship, hate in every act.

And I blame others for my unhappiness. I blame God: where is He? Why hasn't He done anything? Why is He punishing me? I blame my family: it is their fault I married him in the first place. After all, they drummed it in to my psyche that I had to get married when I grew up. And my friends! Oh, they were likely gossiping and chuckling behind my back, realizing I was about to make a mistake but lacking the courage to tell me. And of those who did speak up? Well, they should have tried harder!

¶ I feel violated, taken advantage of, and deliberately exposed to hurt and harm.

My spirit is broken; I have lost sight of who I am. My talents and resources are devalued and unappreciated. I get no credit for any good thing but bear the brunt of every perceived wrong. I believe I have no protection or recourse for absolution. Wallowing in self-pity, I lose my essence.

🍴 **I have lost my vision.**

So concerned with simply surviving, I forget all that God made me to be and to do and I slowly and surely begin to die.

A marriage paradise, on the other hand, would be a place where:

🍴 **I am loved unconditionally.**

Where I have my personal space, but am never lonely because I am secure in the love of my husband. I know he will stand by me through "thick or thin". My husband lavishes me with affection: I'm kissed, cuddled, hugged, smiled at, and appreciated.

🍴 **I'm treated with respect and kindness.**

My opinions matter; my body is treasured; my dreams are respected and supported. My husband encourages me to thrive and supports me in discovering my purpose. I am secure in who I am.

🍴 **I dream big and am encouraged to express my vision.**

My marriage relationship inspires and challenges me to be who I should be and to get where I should in life. Overall, I am happy and content.

Believe me, when I finished this little exercise, I determined to make my marriage a paradise-or as close to one as I could. Now, looking back over the last fifteen years of married life, I am happy to say that my marriage is indeed a paradise.

Many wives have asked me over the years how it is that my marriage is so happy, and so I decided to write this book in an attempt to answer that question.

A happy marriage isn't something you can just wish into existence: it doesn't just happen. Like everything else it takes work and that's what this book is about. It's about what you can do to make your marriage work.

I don't claim to have all the answers to every marital problem, but I do know where to find them- the Bible. That's what the focus is here, I'm sharing with you the Biblical principles I have successfully applied to my marriage and showing you how you too can create your own marriage paradise using the same principles.

I've written about what a wife can do to improve and make her marriage successful. So, this book is written specifically for women- although men could learn a thing or two. The advice and tips here are only limited by the fact that it takes not only the wife but the husband too to make a happy marriage. So, for the wife who wants to do her part to create the marriage of her dreams- this was written specially for you.

But first, I want you to know that **anyone can have a successful marriage.** *Anyone*—and that includes you. All you need to do is follow the right recipe.

Note that I said, the "right recipe". Having the right recipe for a dish is important because the right recipe gives you the formula for making your dish work: what ingredients you need and in what quantities, the methods for preparation, and so on. The right recipe gives you guidelines for making your dish a success.

Speaking of recipes, there's one for just about everything: Coco-Cola, soap, hairspray … marriage--and yes, I did just say marriage. If you want your marriage to be a paradise, there is a formula—a right recipe—you need to follow.

Ready for the recipe? Here goes!

The Recipe

From the Kitchen Of: Heaven
Serves: 2
Cook Time: As long as it takes
Difficulty Level: Beginner

Ingredients:
+ God
+Love
+Honour
+Lovemaking
+Commitment

Directions:
Start with the right relationship with God. Then pour in an endless supply of love and honour, knead with commitment and don't skimp on the spice.

Tip:

If mix is tough, just add more of each ingredient. Don't stop until you get the right consistency.

The Marriage Recipe

Ingredients:

+God
+Love
+Honour
+Lovemaking
+Commitment

God

With God all things are possible. (Matthew 19:26)

Every recipe has that one ingredient that defines the dish, a main ingredient without which it would cease to be a recipe for that kind of dish. For example, melon soup would not be melon soup if there were no melons in it and carrot cake would not be carrot cake if it didn't contain carrots.

The recipe for marriage also has its own main ingredient: God. Just as flour is the base ingredient in a cake recipe and must go in first, before the butter or eggs, so God is the base ingredient in a recipe for a successful marriage.

Why Is God So Important in Marriage?

1. ***Because He administers and upholds the marriage covenant.***

My wedding day is a day I'll never forget: I remember all the pomp of the ceremony- my beautiful gown, wonderfully done makeup and hair, the lovely music, smiling faces of my family and friends... but the most important thing I remember- and it is indeed the highlight of that day- was the part where Ossy and I said our vows. At that moment we entered a covenant with each other and with God. God stood as the Ultimate witness and as the Supreme official- marriage is His institution so it has His authority backing it-

So that day, besides the marriage certificate the priest handed to us, I got a spiritual certificate of union signed by God:

> *Yet you say, "For what reason?" Because the Lord has been witness between you and the wife of your youth, with whom you have dealt treacherously; yet she is your companion and your wife by covenant. (Malachi 2:14)*

This covenant with God and with each other is what makes marriage powerful; it's what distinguishes marriage from two people of the opposite sex just living together. A union without this covenant relationship, in reality, means nothing, because nothing binds either party.

2. *Because He is the expert on marriage.*

Marriage is God's idea. It is His design that a man leaves his father and his mother and cleaves to a woman, and that they become one flesh (Gen. 2:24).

If you wanted to know how a thing works or how to repair a faulty piece of equipment, wouldn't you rather go to the manufacturer or authorized dealer? I know I would, and that's why when I needed to have a new inverter set installed, I waited for the company's engineer to come. I didn't try to do it myself. Even when the lights went out and the generator wouldn't come on, I patiently (well maybe not so patiently!) waited until the engineer showed up.

Why? Because he was the expert; he had the know-how and I had no clue what to do. Besides, if I used someone other than the company-approved engineer, I would lose my warranty. Why would the company insist on using their own engineers? Because they know the company's product; they know and work with the manufacturer's manual. So, I let the engineer set up my inverter, show me how to keep it working, and gladly took his card so I could call him if I had any trouble. And you can be sure that I am following his instructions; to do otherwise will damage the inverter.

Just as I needed that engineer for my inverter, I need God to set up my marriage and keep it running. As Scripture says, *"Unless the Lord builds the house, those who build it labour in vain" (Ps 127.1).*

3.   *Because His involvement strengthens the marriage bond.*

Scripture tells us that, *A person standing alone can be attacked and defeated, but two can stand back to back and conquer. Three are even better, for a triple-braided cord is not easily broken (Ecclesiastes 4:12 NLT).*

This verse, when applied to marriage, looks like this:

Me + my husband+ God = a triple-braided cord!

A triple-braided cord. I can relate to this image. I have a head full of beautiful and difficult-to- manage kinky hair. I often wear it in two or three- twists, and I've found that the three-strand twists last the longest. Just as a triple-braided cord makes a hairstyle last longer, so having God in the center of the marriage relationship strengthens the marriage.

4.   *Because adding God enhances, preserves and protects my marriage.*

Like I said earlier, God is the main ingredient in my recipe. But besides seeing God in this recipe as the defining ingredient, I also liken Him in my marriage to salt in my recipe. To illustrate this, I'll be drawing parallels between how I use salt in my cooking and how God in my marriage mirrors that:

First thing salt does in my cooking is **enhance** the flavor of whatever dish I am making. I remember learning just how important the right amount of salt was to my cooking growing up. I learned that it didn't matter if I had the choicest ingredients or the best methods, without some salt, especially in the soups, my food lacked flavour.

Recently, I watched an episode of Chopped, and one contestant lost because she had left out the salt in one of her entrees. All the judges agreed her dishes and presentation were otherwise perfect, but that one dish without salt put her out of the competition- salt is important.

Before I show you how that relates to God in my marriage, I'll like to give a quick definition of the word enhance. According to the dictionary[3], to enhance is *'to intensify, increase, further improve the quality, value or extent of'*. That's what salt does, it works with the already existing ingredients and makes them better.

Relating this to God, when I add Him into my marriage, I give Him the opportunity to improve the quality of my marriage. How is that? He helps me become the kind of woman and wife He wants me to be and gives me the ability to do the things I need to do to make my marriage succeed. How does He do that? By giving me access to His power, wisdom and resources.

Another use of salt in food is for preservation and protection. In my pantry, you'll probably find a couple of tins of sardines, corned beef and olives amongst other things. What do they all have in common? They're ingredients all preserved in salt. Why do we preserve stuff? Because we want them to last longer and do so without getting spoilt. We use salt for preserving food because most germs cannot survive in a very salty environment. In that environment, the germs become dehydrated and die or become temporarily inactive. So, salt not only keeps my food for longer but protects it from potentially harmful micro-organisms.

Like salt, when I put God in my marriage, I'm creating an environment designed to promote the longevity of my marriage and deter anything that could harm or destroy my marriage. In other words, with God, my marriage, is better protected and preserved.

How Do I Add God to My Marriage?

1. *I make Jesus my Lord and Saviour.*

This is key. Without a personal relationship with Jesus, I cannot have God in my life, let alone my marriage. The only way to God is through Jesus.

> *Jesus said to him, "I am the way, the truth, and the life. No one comes to the Father except through Me." (John 14:6)*

Making Jesus my Lord and Saviour started with believing in Him and praying a prayer of confession like the one below:

> Heavenly Father, I come to You in the Name of the Lord Jesus. I admit that I have not been living right and that I am not right with You, I want to be right with You. Please forgive me of all my sins. The Bible says if I confess that "Jesus is Lord," with my mouth and in my heart believe that God raised Him from the dead, I will be saved (Rom. 10:9). I confess with my mouth and I believe with my heart that Jesus is the Lord and Savior of my life. Thank You for saving me!
>
> In Jesus' name I pray. Amen.

With that prayer, I became a child of God: where before I was in enmity to God, I am now a part of His kingdom.

> *He has delivered us from the power of darkness and conveyed us into the kingdom of the Son of His love (Colossians 1:13)*
>
> *But now in Christ Jesus you who once were far off have been brought near by the blood of Christ. (Ephesians 2:13)*
>
> *But God, who is rich in mercy, because of His great love with which He loved us, even when we were dead in trespasses, made us alive together with Christ (by grace you have been saved), and raised us up together, and made us sit*

> *together in the heavenly places in Christ Jesus, 7 that in the*
> *ages to come He might show the exceeding riches of His grace*
> *in His kindness toward us in Christ Jesus. (Ephesians 2: 4-7)*

> *Therefore you are no longer a slave but a son, and if a son,*
> *then an heir of God through Christ. (Galatians 4:7)*

With my new status, I now have access to all that God is and all that He has. That access gives me the potential to create a good marriage.

But making Jesus my Lord and Saviour requires more than just praying a prayer. It's not that simple. While I had little problem accepting and making Jesus Savior of my life, making Him Lord was another matter. That's something that I constantly must do, every day. Making Him Lord means giving Him authority and power over me and all that concerns me, including my marriage. It means subjecting myself to His will rather than my own and following His dictates--which brings us to the next way I bring God into my marriage.

2. *I obey His Word, follow His principles.*

God drew the blueprint for marriage, so if I want to build mine according to His standard, I must work with His design, which is outlined in the Bible. I add God to my marriage by making the Bible the only and final authority I accept with regards to how I live as a child of God and as a wife. The Bible is the source for my job description, my expectations, my policies, beliefs, and actions as it concerns my marriage.

3. *I listen to godly counsel.*

Scripture tells me that to be wise I must surround myself with the wise:

> *He that walks with wise shall be wise; but a companion of*
> *fools shall be destroyed. (Proverbs 13:20)*

Growing up, I was told that experience was the best teacher. I agree with that cliché somewhat, only I've modified it to be "experience can be a good teacher, but the experience doesn't always have to be mine." I have come to value learning from those who have accomplished the things that I am trying to accomplish: like having a long and happy marriage and having a marriage where our union becomes even better with time.

One of my first marital role models was a senior colleague at work- I fondly call her 'Sotie', at the time she'd been married for thirteen years. I would listen to her literally gush about her husband : how fantastic he was, how much they loved each other, what an awesome father he was, how well they complemented each other…, I would watch her when she spoke to him on the phone: she would beam and blush, flirt…and then I would watch them together- he would often come to pick her up from work and they would almost always be together for every wedding, birthday party, christening and every event we attended- and they would be giggling, whispering into each other's ears and all touchy-touchy like two lovestruck teenagers. I wanted that- I wanted a marriage that didn't grow dull with time, I wanted to have that kind of friendship with my husband! So, I peppered Sotie with questions and learnt from her practical examples: she gave me my first real- life example of a happy Christian home.

I remember how one year she planned a valentine tryst for her husband and made sure I did the same for mine. So, we went shopping for scented candles, aromatic oils, love cards (we bought the blank ones, so we could write in our own words), lingerie and some CDs- Teddy Pendergrass for me- then when we got back she told me it was important to always find time to create special moments for Ossy and I. That was what that whole shopping trip was about, she showed me how with a little thought and creativity I could create a 'five star' date even on a budget.

Over the years, I've sought godly counsel about marriage from my pastors, attended marriage seminars, read books on healthy marriages, and listened to many teachings on marriage. I ask questions and seek guidance from older, happy couples. I surround myself with godly sources of advice and information that will help me make my marriage work.

I believe that many a marriage could have been saved if the parties concerned had sought the godly counsel of a Christian marriage counsellor during times of crisis. I'm not talking about complaining and throwing pity parties with a few friends. I'm talking about seeking guidance and wisdom from someone trained to give marital counselling with the intention of solving or working through a problem. This is nothing to be ashamed of. According to Scripture, it is wise to get help when we need it:

> Through pride and presumption come nothing but strife, but (skillful and godly) wisdom is with those who welcome (well-advised) counsel. (Proverbs 13:10 AMP)

4. *I pray for my marriage.*

When I pray, I am creating opportunity for the power of God to invade and influence my life. Scripture says:

> ...The earnest prayer of a righteous person has great power and produces wonderful results- James 5:16 (NLT)

Remember how I said that adding God to my marriage enhances and preserves my marriage? Prayer is one way I make that happen. When I pray about my marriage, I am opening a channel for God to come in and help me produce the kind of results I couldn't all by myself. I am partnering with God to create a happy home.

What Prayer Is

What is prayer? It's communication with God. It is my direct line to God. When I pray, I am acknowledging that God is present, that He hears me and that we can relate with each other.

I once heard that a certain young entrepreneur paid a million dollars to have lunch with the richest man in the world at that time-even if that story wasn't true, I still like the principle of it. Let's say it did happen, why would anyone pay so much to have a meal with the wealthiest man on earth? Do you think it would be for the food? I don't think so! If that was me at that table, food would be the furthest thing from my mind. I would come with a list of questions, questions like how did you get to where you are and how can I replicate that in my life? I would show him my goals, show him my work and seek his counsel about what I could do to make it better. That lunch date would be for me a classroom- I would be there to learn new things, to unlearn anything that might be holding me back and to become more, to become better! Can you see that the young man was hungry? So hungry he thought nothing of paying so much to assuage that hunger? Hungry for more! Not food, but knowledge, experience, wisdom, instruction, counsel...!

Sounds like he took a page from the Bible...

> 'Wisdom is supreme. Get wisdom. Yes, though it costs all your possessions, get understanding'- Proverbs 4:7 (WEB)

That's what prayer is, it's my date with God! Imagine that! I get to meet with the all-knowing, all-powerful and all-resourceful God. Unlike any other meeting, meeting with God is a meeting filled with unlimited possibilities. Why? Because, God is limitless- there's no limit to what I can learn, no limit to what I can gain and no limit to what God can do for me -within the context of His will. Why did I add that last bit? Because, God does not operate outside of who He is and the provisions He has made available to me- His will. To know what His will is, I check the Bible, for there God has revealed what His will is. For example, from Scripture God did not give me dominion over any human being, so no matter how sincerely or fervently I pray about it- God will not give me control over my husband. God is truly limitless but paradoxically He is limited by Himself.

So, what are these meetings like? A time to come with a long list of desires for God to fulfill? Nope. Although at first, I did start out that way, I've learnt that God is not my personal vending machine. So, when I pray, it's not about wanting God to fulfill my every wish. Do I bring Him requests? Yes, but that's not the only reason I pray.

Like that young man with the rich patron, I go to God in prayer to release His power into my situation, to gain insight, to gain instruction and correction and I go to God in prayer because He loves me, and I know He's always there for me- to be all that I need.

How does prayer help my marriage?

¶¶ Prayer releases God's power into my home.

And when they had prayed, the place where they were meeting together was shaken [a sign of God's presence]; and they were all filled with the Holy Spirit and began to speak the word of God with boldness and courage. -Acts 4:31(AMP)

When I pray, I open myself to be filled with the Holy Spirit just like all the saints in the Bible. And believe me I need the Holy Spirit. We all do. When Jesus was on earth, everything He was able to do was because of the Holy Spirit.

'...You must know the story of Jesus of Nazareth—why, it has spread through the whole of Judea, beginning with Galilee after the baptism that John proclaimed. You must have heard how God anointed him with the power of the Holy Spirit, of how he went about doing good and healing all who suffered from the devil's power—because God was with him... Acts 10:38(PHILLIPS)

If Jesus needed the Holy Spirit, then surely, I do! It is through the help and power of the Holy Spirit that I can be a good wife, that I can fix any marital problems that might arise and that I can stand against the devil's attack on my marriage. I can't do any of that if God is not with me. And when I pray, I strengthen and maintain my connection with Him- I allow God in the person of the Holy Spirit to be my Helper (Parakletos[4])- *Comforter, Advocate, Intercessor—Counselor, Strengthener, Standby forever. John 14:16 (AMP)*

Power- 'Authority that is given or delegated to a person or body. The ability or capacity to do something or act in a particular way.'[5]

I have power- I have delegated authority. Jesus gave that to me.

"Assuredly, I say to you, whatever you bind on earth will be bound in heaven, and whatever you loose on earth will be loosed in heaven." Matthew 18:18

I have the 'right' to bind and to loose here on earth- but don't get too excited, there's a 'condition' to what that covers. I can't just run around binding and loosening everything willy-nilly 😊. To see the clause, let's see Matthew 18: 18 in a different translation;

Truly I tell you, whatever you forbid and declare to be improper and unlawful on earth must be what is already forbidden in heaven, and whatever you permit and declare proper and lawful on earth must be what is already permitted in heaven-(AMPC)

That's the clause, I can only forbid or allow anything here on earth based on God's will (as it is in heaven). That kills any hopes of being able to bind any football matches, so I can watch Law and Order[6] instead 😊. But seriously though, if I stay within the boundaries of God's Word- the Bible, a realm of endless possibilities is open to me in my marriage.

It is in the place of prayer that I exercise the authority Christ has given me. When I pray, I bring this power to bear on whatever it is I'm praying about. I become a vessel through which God's power can flow. Prayer allows the power of the Holy Spirit flow through me to affect what I'm praying about. So, when I pray for my marriage, I allow the Holy Spirit touch it.

I know that without the power of God in my marriage there's no way I could be happily married for as long as I have. It's because God's in my marriage that it's been protected from harm and one way I've ensured I keep the power flowing into my home is on my knees.

🍴 **Prayer creates an atmosphere where God can teach me, correct me and instruct me.**

The Bible is my primary source for correction and instruction:

'All *scripture is given by inspiration of God, and is profitable for doctrine, for reproof, for correction, for [a]instruction in righteousness, that the man of God may be complete, thoroughly equipped for every good work.- (2 Timothy 3:16-17)*

But the Bible doesn't always give me specific instructions as pertains to my individual life- what I mean by that is that there's no chapter and verse instruction for every detail of my life. For instance, I won't find in the Bible the answer to 'what colour I should paint my house?' or 'which part of town I should live? Will and should the Bible guide my decisions? Yes?!

Using the example of painting my house, while the Bible doesn't say what colour my house should be, it does say I should walk in love towards others. So, if my landlord wants every flat uniformly painted beige on the outside, from the Bible I know, I shouldn't go ahead and paint my porch bright red. And with regards, where to live, from scripture I know I shouldn't be heading towards a part of town known for high rates of crime or debauchery. Why? Because, I wouldn't want to expose my family to corrupting influences.

Don't be fooled by those who say such things, for "bad company corrupts good character."- 1 Corinthians 15:33(NLT)

Sometimes though, it's a bit more difficult to discern what the right thing to do is, sometimes because my emotions are clouding my mind, so I can't see the way or simply because I just don't know what to do. At times like that, praying helps. Praying gives God, the opportunity to speak to me- to instruct me and to correct me where needed.

One example comes to mind. My husband was traveling and somehow missed his connecting flight home. He was at the airport on time, and yet didn't make it to the gate on time. The plane left without him. When he called to let me know, I was peeved; I kept asking, "How did that happen? How come you weren't paying attention?" Then we lost the connection (I think he hung up on me), and I tried calling back, getting angrier and angrier that he wasn't answering.

Finally, I just went to God. 'Lord, can you see what he's doing? He's not picking my calls! And here I've been waiting for him to arrive-- favorite dish prepared, all dolled up, and he goes and misses his flight! To top it up, he's showing no concern about how I must be feeling right now....' on and on I went. The more I griped about it, the worst I felt. I thought I was praying, but what I was really doing was complaining and throwing a pity party for myself- more on that in a bit. Finally, exhausted, I said to God, 'How do I make him understand how I feel, get him to put himself in my shoes?'

And, clear as a bell, the Holy Spirit said, 'How about putting yourself in his shoes first'? Suddenly, I saw the situation differently. My exhausted husband had just come off a fourteen-hour flight. He'd had to wait another four hours for his connecting flight, and he'd missed it. How frustrating that must have been! And there I was, nagging him, thinking only about myself. I wouldn't have wanted to talk to me either.

I immediately sent a loving text to my hubby, telling him I was sorry for being so harsh, and that it was okay he'd missed his flight. I asked if he'd eaten--perhaps he'd want to check into a hotel and get some sleep and fly home the next day. And guess what? He called me right away. Turns out that all the time I had been calling and calling, he'd been at the ticket counter trying to get on another fight, and my calling was only adding to his frustration.

Prayer changed everything—but it wasn't until I stopped complaining and started praying, asking God for wisdom, that He was able to instruct me and give me the tools to turn that situation around.

¶ Prayer strengthens me and gives me peace.

Ever felt frazzled, weak, inadequate, worried and anxious? I have, time and time again. I sometimes worry I'm not achieving a good work-life-balance, or about my husband's safety- recently a close friend, slumped in his hotel room and by the time his wife was able to get the hotel staff to check his room after she'd been unable to reach him, he had passed on. That increased my fears about my husband too (he also travels frequently for business). Many things can press on me from time to time, threatening to rob my peace. But in the place of prayer I not only find the strength to overcome my challenges but also peace for my heart.

> *Don't worry about anything; instead pray about everything.*
> *Tell God what you need, and thank him for all he has done.*
> *Then you will experience God's peace, which exceeds anything*
> *we can understand. His peace will guard your hearts and*
> *minds as you live in Christ Jesus. Philippians 4:9 (NLT)*

That's how I find peace, this peace is not as a result of me playing ostrich (burying my head and hiding from reality) but a knowledge I get in the place of prayer- what's that knowledge? That God has got me covered- that with God I can deal successfully with 'whatever'. How? That in God, I'll get everything I need to overcome my challenges. That's how that peace comes.

Let me explain, remember how I said I got really worried about my husband whenever he travelled- with him being alone in his hotel room? Well, I went to God about it in prayer. So, what happened?

First, God reminded me of His many promises of safety and protection over my household;

The name of the Lord is a strong fortress, the godly run to him and are safe- Proverbs 18:10 (NLT)

And one of my favourite Psalms- Psalm 91

He who dwells in the secret place of the Most High

Shall abide under the shadow of the Almighty.

2 I will say of the Lord, "He is my refuge and my fortress;

My God, in Him I will trust."

3 Surely He shall deliver you from the snare of the [a]fowler

And from the perilous pestilence.

4 He shall cover you with His feathers,

And under His wings you shall take refuge;

His truth shall be your shield and [b]buckler.

5 You shall not be afraid of the terror by night,

Nor of the arrow that flies by day,

6 Nor of the pestilence that walks in darkness,

Nor of the destruction that lays waste at noonday.

7 A thousand may fall at your side,

And ten thousand at your right hand;

But it shall not come near you.

8 Only with your eyes shall you look,

And see the reward of the wicked.

9 Because you have made the Lord, who is my refuge,

Even the Most High, your dwelling place,

10 No evil shall befall you,

Nor shall any plague come near your dwelling;

11 For He shall give His angels charge over you,

To keep you in all your ways.

12 In their hands they shall [c]bear you up,

Lest you [d]dash your foot against a stone.

13 You shall tread upon the lion and the cobra,

The young lion and the serpent you shall trample underfoot.

14 "Because he has set his love upon Me, therefore I will deliver him;

I will [e]set him on high, because he has known My name.

15 He shall call upon Me, and I will answer him;

I will be with him in trouble;

I will deliver him and honor him.

16 With [f]long life I will satisfy him,

And show him My salvation."

Every verse in that Psalm reminds me of God's promise to protect me and mine when we abide under His shadow. And one way I do that is by praying.

In praying about my concerns regarding Ossy's trips, I found comfort and renewed confidence in God's ability to maintain my lot just like He promised;

> *Lord, you alone are my inheritance, my cup of blessing. You guard all that is mine. Psalms 16:5 (NLT)*

But besides the comfort I found in the place of prayer, I also found practical wisdom. See, in the place of prayer, as comfort came, fear left, and with fear gone, God could now instruct my heart. What kind of instruction? Practical stuff.

That I needed to get relevant knowledge in that area and apply it- I needed to answer the question-what could cause sudden death, like in the case of our friend? From my research, I found two major factors that could contribute to sudden unexpected death- poor overall health and stress.

That meant, I had to check up on our health- were we eating healthily, or did I have to make some modifications to our menu? Time for our annual medical checkup- book one and get it done? Time to buy a blood pressure monitor. Exercise? Was exercising at home enough, or was it time to sign up to a gym?

Then about stress? What was the atmosphere at home like? Were we getting enough rest, taking out time to relax? Time to cut down on TV so we could sleep earlier? Or just switch it off so we had better quality time? Plan a vacation? In answering those questions, I could better cooperate with God's protection over my husband and family.

What's my point? When I prayed about my fears God was able to give me tools to overcome them and bring peace to my heart.

⍾ Prayer gives me access to God's mercy

I am not the perfect wife- far from it! I fail every now and then. Why don't I reap the consequences of my failings? Because of God's mercy.

'If we confess our sins, He is faithful and just to forgive us our sins and to cleanse us from all unrighteousness.' – 1John 1:9

'My little children, these things I write to you, so that you may not sin. And if anyone sins, we have an Advocate with the Father, Jesus Christ the righteous'- 1 John 2:1

You have come to Jesus, the one who mediates the new covenant between God and people, and to the sprinkled blood, which speaks of forgiveness instead of crying out for vengeance like the blood of Abel. Hebrews 12:24 (NLT)

When I go to God in prayer, praying over my marriage, I give Jesus the opportunity to mediate for me. He pleads for me, crying mercy, mercy! He intercedes for me, declaring that He has paid the price for my mercy.

Mercy- 'the discretionary power of a judge to pardon someone or to mitigate punishment'[7]

That's what happens when I pray about my marriage- God can use His discretionary power to save me from the natural consequences of my misdemeanors or omissions as a wife.

So when I make mistakes, I run to God and ask Him for forgiveness and for those things I don't even know I'm doing wrong, His mercy still prevails as He leads me to a place where I overcome those shortcomings.

Praying for my marriage releases God's power to work in me and through me, and in and through my husband, and to make our marriage stronger.

I've said a lot about what prayer is and how praying helps my marriage, next I want to share how I pray.

So how do I pray?

Paul says we're to pray always, with all kinds of prayer.

> *Pray at all times (on every occasion, in every season) in the Spirit, with all [manner of] prayer and entreaty. To that end keep alert and watch with strong purpose and perseverance, interceding in behalf of all the saints (God's consecrated people) -Ephesians 6:18 (AMPC)*

I love this verse. Why? Because it shows me how even in prayer, God celebrates individuality and allows each of us to be ourselves. So, I don't have to try like to pray exactly like anyone else, or limit myself to anyone's one idea of how, where or when I should pray. Neither do I have to restrict myself to one method or type of prayer. I can take examples from the Bible and make them mine.

So even as I share my 'how' of prayer, remember that you don't have to limit yourself to what I'm sharing, search scriptures for examples that would suit you.

Here's how I pray...

- I have a conversation with God. I imagine Him standing or sitting across from me and just talk to Him and wait for His response/s. Is that allowed, is it scriptural? Yes. The Bible gives examples of men having conversations with God- Abraham, Moses. These men would talk to God 'face to face'. Of Moses, God said in Numbers 12:6-8 (NLT)

"When there is a prophet among you,

I, the Lord, reveal myself to them in visions,
I speak to them in dreams.
But this is not true of my servant Moses;
he is faithful in all my house.
With him I speak face to face,
clearly and not in riddles;
he sees the form of the Lord."

- I write my prayers (I keep a prayer journal) and record what God tells me. How do I know this can be a form of prayer? Because I have many examples of the saints of old writing down their prayers- the book of Psalms is full of David's prayers, I have examples of Paul's written prayers in his epistles.

- I pray silently. Does God hear my thoughts? Yes, He does.

O Lord, You have searched me and known me.
You know my sitting down and my rising up;
You understand my thought afar off.- Psalm 139:1-2

- I pray in other tongues:

'And they were all filled with the Holy Spirit and began to speak with other tongues, as the Spirit gave them utterance.'- Acts 2:4

For he who speaks in a tongue does not speak to men but to God, for no one understands him; however, in the spirit he speaks mysteries.

I like praying in tongues, especially because when I pray in tongues, I know I'm allowing the Holy Spirit pray for me by giving me utterance. And oh what a blessing to have God give me His own language, His own sounds, to pray without any human limitations!

> *"Also, the Spirit helps us. We are very weak, but the Spirit helps us with our weakness. We don't know how to pray as we should, but the Spirit himself speaks to God for us. He begs God for us, speaking to him with feelings too deep for words. God already knows our deepest thoughts. And he understands what the Spirit is saying, because the Spirit speaks for his people in the way that agrees with what God wants"- Romans 8:26-27 (ERV)*

> <u>*For if I pray in an [unknown] tongue, my spirit [by the Holy Spirit within me] prays,*</u> *but my mind is unproductive*

[it bears no fruit and helps nobody]. (Emphasis mine)- 1 Corinthians 14:14 (AMPC)

Like I said, when I pray, I don't restrict myself to any one manner of prayer. But even as I celebrate the diversity that can be found in the place of prayer, I must mention that prayer holds certain constants - without them, I couldn't call whatever I deem prayer, prayer. That informs the next bit...

What's Important when I pray?

1. That I pray in the Name of Jesus and enter God's presence on the premise of Jesus' finished works.

This is the most important factor of prayer- the Name of Jesus and Redemption. The name of Jesus is the 'PIN' or the authorized signature on my heavenly account. In the natural, I could have a million dollars (that would be nice 😊) in my bank account but without a duly signed cheque or the right 'PIN' (personal identification number) to my ATM card, I wouldn't be able to access that money.

As a child of God, I have invaluable treasure and benefits and it is the Name of Jesus that gives me the access to receiving or experiencing any one of them. I cannot expect to receive answers to any prayers I make for my marriage and indeed anything else if I fail to pray using Jesus' name.

> *'At that time you won't need to ask me for anything. I tell you the truth, you will ask the Father directly, and he will grant your request because you use my name. You haven't done this before. Ask, using my name, and you will receive, and you will have abundant joy.'- John 16:23-24(NLT)*

The time Jesus spoke about is now- after His death, burial and resurrection. This- now, today is when I must make all requests to the Father in Jesus Name. I not only make my requests in this precious name, I enter God's presence based on what Jesus did for me. It is on the basis of redemption that I can pray and that my prayers are effective.

'Now all of us can come to the Father through the same Holy Spirit because of what Christ has done for us.'- Ephesians 2:18 (NLT)

And so, dear brothers and sisters,[a] we can boldly enter heaven's Most Holy Place because of the blood of Jesus. Hebrews 10:19 (NLT)

2. I pray according to God's Word. I've said before that what I can pray for is limited to what's available to me in the Bible. That's one aspect of praying according to God's Word. It means that I limit my requests, desires, expectations and even exercising my authority as a believer to what Scripture says I can. When I do that, my prayers are effective;

   'But if you remain in Me and My words remain in you, you may ask for anything you want, and it shall be granted!' - John 15:7 (NLT)

The word of God remaining in me implies that I know it, spend time with it and obey it. If I do all that, then I would know the will of God and if I know the will of God then my prayers would be based on His will and therefore my prayers will be answered.

And this is the confidence which we have before Him:

That God Hears Our Prayers

... that if we request anything according to His will, He hears us. And if we know that He hears us— whatever we request— we know that we have the requests which we have requested from Him. 1 John 5: 14-15 (DLNT)

God's Will...

I have said a couple of times that God's Will = God's Word = The Bible, but that's not the only part of God's will. The Bible will give me God's general will for my life and marriage like how a wife should treat her husband, how a woman can build a successful home etc. but will not give me specifics about my marriage as relating to Ossy and I. Here's what I mean, and I've said so earlier- I can't find my husband's name or mine in the Bible. I won't find a verse that reads 'say this or that to Ossy in a particular situation or that tells me what time based or location-based action to take with respect to my husband. That kind of information or instruction is what I call God's specific will. Let me give you an example from the Bible;

The Macedonian Call

Now when they had gone through Phrygia and the region of Galatia, they were forbidden by the Holy Spirit to preach the word in [a]Asia. After they had come to Mysia, they tried to go into Bithynia, but the [b]Spirit did not permit them. So passing by Mysia, they came down to Troas. And a vision appeared to Paul in the night. A man of Macedonia stood and pleaded with him, saying, "Come over to Macedonia and help us." Now after he had seen the vision, immediately we sought to go to Macedonia, concluding that the Lord had called us to preach the gospel to them.

The above passage is an account of something that happened during Paul's second missionary journey. Based on God's 'general will' (*"Go into all the world and preach the gospel to every creature" – Mark 16:15*). Paul made plans to take the gospel to Phrygia, and Galatia, but here we see that the Holy Spirit said no to that, and the same thing happened when Paul and his companions tried to go to Bithynia. But you might ask- 'wasn't it God's will that the people in that area got saved'? Certainly, it was. But at that time, that was not God's specific will for Paul. God wanted Paul in Macedonia. And the reason Paul was able to discern God's specific will for him for that season? Because he was in constant fellowship with the Holy Spirit.

That's what praying does for me, it keeps me in fellowship with God and if I'm constantly relating with Him, then He can give me details of His personal will for my life and marriage in real time.

The other aspect of praying according to God's Word, involves praying in God's words. What do I mean? I mean that when I pray, I use words from the Bible and bring them before God.

For example, when praying for my husband I might use a scripture like 1 Chronicles 4:10

'Jabez cried out to the God of Israel, saying, "Oh that You would indeed bless me and enlarge my border [property], and that Your hand would be with me, and You would keep me from evil so that it does not hurt me!" And God granted his request.'

And using this scripture, I would pray something like this:

'Heavenly Father, thank you for Your unfailing love for me and my family. Thank you for your amazing blessings, too numerous to count and thank You for your Word.

You said Lord that all scripture is for my benefit- to teach, correct and instruct- so I know that the examples I find in Your Word are for me to learn from and because I know that You never change, whatever You did for the saints of old You can do for me too.

So Father, just like Jabez prayed, I make the same request for Ossy- Dear Lord, please bless Ossy and enlarge his borders- cause increases in his business, more customers, more dedicated and hard-working staff, more investment opportunities…., put Your hand upon him Lord and protect him from all evil!'

In Jesus Name

While using my own words is okay when I pray, using God inspired words is better. Why? Think of it, whose words can never be wrong? God's! Don't get me wrong, I use my own words to talk to God and it's a beautiful thing to express myself in my way to my Father but I'm saying, when I use words from the Bible, it's more difficult to pray amiss.

To pray according to God's Word mandates that I know the Word for myself, particularly about whatever it is I want to pray about. So, the first thing I do before I pray is find the scripture/s that covers what I'm praying about. When I am armed with that, then I can be confident in my prayers.

3. I make my prayers specific- I ask for what I want.

> "*Ask*, and it will be given to you; seek, and you will find; knock, and it will be opened to you. For everyone who asks receives, and he who seeks finds, and to him who knocks it will be opened. Or what man is there among you who, if his son asks for bread, will give him a stone? Or if he asks for a fish, will he give him a serpent? If you then, being evil, know how to give good gifts to your children, how much more will your Father who is in heaven give good things to those who ask Him!"- Matthew 7:7-11

God wants me to ask Him for what I want. Did you notice how He was specific about what had been asked? Bread, fish? This wasn't the same as just asking for food -what kind of food?

So, when I'm making my requests I'm specific too- for example when I want to ask God to bless my marriage, I am specific about the kind of blessings I want to experience. I ask for increased affection between my husband and I, I ask for unity, for peace…

4. I pray in faith.

Faith- Belief, trust, and loyalty to a person or thing.[8]

When I pray, I pray trusting God, I pray believing God. I believe that God is who He says He is, that God has done what He said He has done and will do all He says He will do for me. I believe that when I pray according to God's will, God hears me and because He hears me I know I have my requests.

> …*It's impossible to please God apart from faith. And why? Because anyone who wants to approach God must believe*

both that he exists and that he cares enough to respond to those who seek him. – Hebrews 11:6 (MSG)

God cares for me! He's concerned about every aspect of my life including my marriage.

I am your God and will take care of you until you are old and your hair is gray. I made you and will care for you; I will give you help and rescue you.- Isaiah 46: 4 (GNT)

I believe that with all my heart! It is with this confidence, this attitude, this complete resting in God and His Word that I pray.

In Hebrews 11, I see another definition of faith.

Now faith is the substance of things hoped for, the evidence of things not seen- Hebrews 11:1

What's the substance of the things I hope for in my marriage? What evidence do I have that my desires will come to pass? It is my confidence in God. This is the basis of my faith. I believe that there's nothing impossible with God.

That's how the saints of old recorded in the faith hall of fame in Hebrews 11 lived- Abel, Enoch, Noah, Abraham, Sarah, Isaac, Jacob, Joseph, Moses... They all put absolute trust in God. Because they did, nothing God promised seemed unattainable, it didn't matter how contrary the circumstances around looked, if God had said it they believed it! When God promised a child, not even menopause could shake Sarah's faith in God.

So, when I go to Him in prayer, I'm not doubting his ability or willingness to help me. And God is so good, He even gives me help in believing- I don't even have to depend on myself to get faith. God gave it to me as a gift.

For I say, through the grace given unto me, to every man that is among you, not to think of himself more highly than he

ought to think; but to think soberly, according as God hath
dealt to every man the measure of faith.- Romans 12:3 (KJV)

God has given me the ability to believe in Him, the ability to trust Him. So, I pray in faith! I never consider that my prayers are not heard because God said that He hears me when I pray.

"For the eyes of the Lord are on the righteous, And His ears
are open to their prayers;" – 1 Peter 3:12

God said He cares for me, so much that not even a single strand of my hair falls without Him taking notice.

"Indeed, the very hairs of your head are all numbered. Do not
fear; you are more valuable than many sparrows."

God catches my tears too and stores them.

"You number my wanderings; Put my tears into Your bottle;
Are they not in Your book?" Psalm 56:8

"Therefore I say to you, whatever things you ask when you
pray, believe that you receive them, and you will have
them." – Mark 11:24

When I focus my heart on scriptures like these, faith comes! Just like scripture says, the more I hear about God, the more I know about God, the more faith comes…

"So then faith comes by hearing, and hearing by the word of
God."- Romans 10:17

So far, I've talking about how important it is that I pray in faith. And my focus has been on faith here as being in God and being the confidence, I have towards Him- faith as being expressed as a belief or attitude regarding God. But that's not all there is to faith…

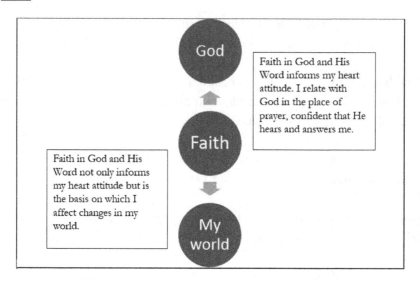

Permit me to digress a bit here from prayer. I wouldn't have done justice on the concept of faith if I don't. I don't just need faith to pray, I need faith to change the circumstances of my life.

The work of faith...

What do I mean? Let's see a few scriptures to illustrate;

> "So Jesus said to them, "Because of your unbelief; for assuredly, I say to you, *if you have faith* as a mustard seed, *you will say* to this mountain, 'Move from here to there,' and it will move; and *nothing will be impossible for you*."- Matthew 17:20

Please note the underlined phrases, paraphrasing- 'if I have faith, then I will say'... (keep that thought in mind).

> "So Jesus answered and said to them, "*Have faith in God*. For assuredly, I say to you, *whoever says* to this mountain, 'Be removed and be cast into the sea,' and does not doubt in his heart, *but believes that those things he* says will be done, he will have whatever he says."- Mark 11: 22-23

Again, mark those underlined words. There's a common thread here- faith is associated with speaking. This is how the physical world gets affected. By the words I speak. Faith cannot just stay silent in my heart, it must speak. This is true for every believer, just as it was for the saints of old.

> *"And since we have the same spirit of faith, according to what is written, "I believed and therefore I spoke," we also believe and therefore speak,"- 2 Corinthians 4:13*

From Genesis to Revelation, we see God and His saints speaking – everything that God did was first spoken about. For thousands of years before Christ came, God spoke about redemption. From the garden of Eden and through the prophets, God declared what would be. As a believer I should be no different.

So, faith involves finding Bible verses that show me what I want to experience in my marriage and speaking them daily. I personalize them and make them part of my daily faith confessions. For example, I say (this taken from Prov. 31-10-12):

I am a wife of noble character, I am worth far more than rubies.

My husband has full confidence in me and lacks nothing of value.

I bring him good, not harm all the days of my life.

As I speak these words of faith, two things happen. First, my confidence in God's Word in this respect grows. Speaking my faith is akin to me planting those words in my heart, and that's a prerequisite to the Word bearing fruit-yielding results. Second, the Holy Spirit illuminates my mind so that I see how to apply God's Word to my peculiar situation. The process goes like this:

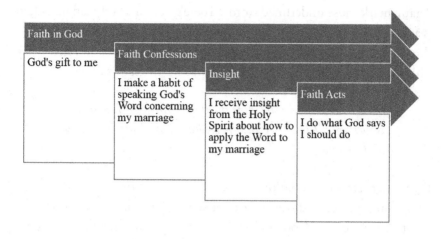

So, for instance, I want my husband to have confidence in me, to trust me and not keep secrets from me. This is what it looks like for me to walk by faith in this area.

First, I go to scripture to see if God has promised me anything like that- faith only works with the Word of God. God will not honour faith in anything else. I can only expect God to give me what He has made provision for. So, I check, and I find a scripture like Proverbs 31:10-12--

Who can find a virtuous wife?

For her worth is far above rubies.

The heart of her husband safely trusts her;

So he will have no lack of gain.

She does him good and not evil

All the days of her life.

-- and daily make confessions, like the example I gave earlier. As I continually do that, the Holy Spirit begins to show me corrections I need to make or actions I need to take to bring that confession to pass. For example, He may remind me not to break my husband's confidence or show me that I need to ease up on a critical spirit. The Holy Spirit shows me from the Bible what kind of wife I need to be for my husband to have confidence in me.

The last part of this process of walking by faith is for me to obey, to do as the Holy Spirit has taught me.

Here's a quick summary of what I've said so far about faith:

- I need faith for my prayers to be effective.

- As a believer, I already have faith; God gave it to me as a gift.

- I need faith to effect change in my circumstances and I make my faith work by speaking and acting on God's Word.

5. I wait patiently for the answers to my prayers

> *That you do not become sluggish but imitate those who through faith and patience inherit the promises. - Hebrews 6:12*

Prayer is not a magic wand- when I pray about my marriage or anything else in my life, the manifestations of the answers are not always immediate. Sometimes it takes some time. Why shouldn't that worry me? Because if I'm sure what I'm asking for is within God's will for me then I am assured that I shall have it.

> *"And whatever things you ask in prayer, believing, you <u>will</u> receive."- Matthew 21:21*

> *"And whatever you ask in My name, that I <u>will</u> do, that the Father may be glorified in the Son."- John 14:13*

> *"If you abide in Me, and My words abide in you, you will ask what you desire, and it <u>shall</u> be done for you."- John 15:7*

Note the words 'will' and 'shall' in the verses above, they connote 'in the future'. They introduce the concept of time to the answering of prayers.

Time... "plan, schedule, or arrange when (something) should happen or be done"[9]

This scheduled time could be in seconds, minutes, hours, days, weeks, months or even years. In whatever case, the same principle applies- I must be patient.

> *But let patience have its perfect work, that you may be perfect and complete, lacking nothing.* -James 1:4

When praying for my marriage, what do I pray about?

I pray about everything- I pray about me, I pray about my husband and I pray about everything and anything that affects us. For example, most mornings when I open my eyes my husband is the first thing I see, which makes me smile, so I thank God for the man He gave me, for the peace in our home, and our hope for the future. Then later in the day, if I notice a crease on my husband's forehead (usually while going over his business accounts), I talk to God about his work. Here's the thing, as long as I keep my marriage in prayers, God has the opportunity to influence it.

And the great thing about prayer? I can never have excess, too much doesn't ruin things. It is impossible to pray too much! Rather, prayer positions me to get what I need from God- sometimes what I need is wisdom, sometimes grace to be more patient😊, or a change of perspective.

So when it comes to praying for my marriage, I pray about whatever is on my mind, and wait for God's answer.

I found a poem by an unknown author in my Church bulletin[10] recently that aptly describes what I believe prayer is about;

"I know not what methods rare,
But this I know- God answers prayers.

I know that He has given His Word,
Which tells me prayer is always heard,
And will be answered, soon or late,
And so I pray and calmly wait.
I know not if blessing sought
Will come in just the way I thought,
But leave my prayers with Him alone,
Whose will is wiser than my own.
Assured that He will grant my quest,
Or send some answer far more blest"

This chapter has been about giving God place in my marriage- Because I've put God in my marriage the center of my focus changes from my husband to God. I don't look to Ossy to complete me or give to me that inner sense of security, I look to God. I don't expect my husband to be perfect or to be able to provide for my every need, I have God for that. I am not guided by my feelings or the feelings of my husband either, God becomes my compass- His principles determine my choices.

By including God in my relationship, I open the door to God's resources- I gain access to grace- strength, undeserved blessings, abilities, power, insight…. - and mercy that helps me create the marriage I dream of.

As I let God help me, I'm growing into the woman and wife He made me to be. As I look back over the years, I know that I couldn't have created a happy home without God's help. It has been this main ingredient that is responsible for all my successes and that has helped me overcome my failures.

If like me, you're ready to move beyond your own limitations and get supernatural help, then put God into your marriage mix and with that in place, let's add in the rest of the ingredients necessary to make our marriages work.

Chef Tips:

✓ If you haven't yet made Jesus your personal Lord and Saviour, do so and give him Lordship over your marriage.

✓ Seek expert Christian counselling if your marriage is in crisis-unresolved and long lasting conflicts, abuse of any kind, threat of divorce or separation, infidelity…;

- talk to your pastor or church marriage counsellor

- attend a Christian marriage seminar; read books to help your marriage.

✓ Create your own faith confessions for your marriage, using God's Word. Here are a few scriptures to get you started: Proverbs 12:4, Proverbs 5:18-19, Ecc. 5:22-24, 1 Peter 3:1-3, and Eph. 5:22-24)

The Marriage Recipe

Ingredients:

+God

+Love
+Honour
+Lovemaking
+Commitment

Love

Love never fails. -1 Corinthians 13:8

In every dish, there's that ingredient that holds all the other stuff together; I call it the binding agent. In our local soups it's called the thickener, like when I add Ofor to my Oha soup[11], cocoyam to my native soup, or eggs to my cake recipe. Without these binders, my dishes don't turn out right. My soups are watery and the cake flat.

The binding ingredient in this recipe for marriage is love. Without love, you cannot have a great or even good marriage.

What is love?

Love is 'strong affection for another arising out of kinship or personal ties'[12] . Love is expressed in different ways and for different reasons. But as relating to my marriage, my definition and blueprint for love is found in 1 Corinthians 13 (AMP), which is often called the love chapter. Let's look at how God defines love in this passage.

Love Endures Long and Is Patient and Kind (V. 4)

I started cooking when I was ten. Through the years, I've been burned, cut, and bruised while making meals. I've had culinary failures. But none of these challenges ever stopped me from cooking the next time. And it's not because I love cooking, because I don't. At first, I kept cooking out of a sense of duty and then as a wife I cook because I am passionate about making sure my family is well-fed. I want to make sure that they eat healthy and tasty meals. That's my purpose when it comes to cooking. I won't be swayed from my goal. I don't let fatigue, a shortage of resources, or even my mood stop me. I try out new recipes, watch food channels (I know ☺...), spend time in the kitchen, and keep on cooking. In other words, I endure in cooking for my family.

Endurance is not a word I would normally like because it sounds like putting up with hard or harsh conditions. But that's not what it means in the context of love. According to *Strong's* concordance, *endurance* is "the characteristic of a man who is un-swerved from his deliberate purpose and his loyalty to faith and piety by even the greatest trials and sufferings."[13] So, the focus of this word is not on trials or sufferings (though there might be some--and I don't mean allowing violence or abuse of any kind) but on being faithful, persistent, in love. In marriage it means loving my husband no matter what obstacles, hindrances, or setbacks I may face.

Before we got married, Ossy and I agreed on certain terms; one of them was that divorce was not an option. We agreed we would do everything it took to make our union work, and to never quit on each other and our marriage. Enduring in love makes us true to that agreement. So, when as a newlywed, I was advised to prepare and protect myself for the eventuality of a divorce, I refused my friend's counsel and other advice in that same vein. Sadly, I lost that friendship. Being loyal to our beliefs about marriage can be costly, but God expects us to endure in love—to be unmoved from that which we have purposed (to build a strong and loving marriage that lasts a lifetime).

According to 1 Corinthians 13, enduring in love involves having an attitude of patience and kindness. In other words, my attitude toward my husband matters. I am to treat him with kindness and patience. Loving my husband means having an unwavering commitment to make my marriage succeed and to have the right attitude along the way.

Patience- the capacity to accept or tolerate delay, problems, or suffering without becoming annoyed or anxious.[14] Hmmm. As a young bride, one of the things I had older couples I spoke to say to me over and over again was "marriage cannot succeed without tolerance". They were right!

One time, I read about a couple who got divorced because one partner squeezed the toothpaste from the middle and not all the way from the bottom. Now that's an extreme case but here's the point, if I don't watch it and allow little annoyances pile up they could eventually become a source of conflict between Ossy and I. So how do I avoid that? By being tolerant? How do I do that? I don't let the unimportant stuff annoy me. I don't mind 'losing the battle to win the war'[15]

Let me give you an example of what I mean; when I stay up late, I tend to get peckish so will often go fix myself a snack. If Ossy is up, I would ask him if he would want a snack too. Nine out of ten times he would say no and then when I come back with snacks, he would eat half of it. That used to make me peeved. What changed? I learned to be more tolerant. Sure, it would've been great if Ossy decided before I went to make snacks whether he wanted any. But it's not a major infraction, it's just one of his little quirks. Being tolerant means that I learn to overlook that and work with it. So now when I make midnight snacks, I make them for two and if it turns out that he really doesn't want any, I can always refrigerate what's left over.

Kindness- 'the quality of being friendly, generous and considerate'[16]

Loving my husband means that I am my husband's friend. That means that it's my responsibility to accept him for who he is, to be loyal, to encourage him, to treat him with courtesy and to help him. I picture what I would want in a friend and I become that friend to Ossy.

Being Ossy's friend is not all there is to being kind to him. I also don't skimp on being affectionate or on doing nice things for him. Like helping him pack his travel bags and leaving little mementos for him to find. Preparing his favourite dish every now and then or giving him a foot massage.

Love Never Is Envious Nor Boils Over With Jealousy (V. 4)

Before I got married, I didn't think this would ever be an issue. I couldn't imagine being envious towards my husband. But I was wrong. How was I envious of him? By wishing we could change places, even for a moment.

Ossy has a steady personality. He's content and doesn't over analyze things. I can't remember him fretting. Even in the face of crisis, he's able to sleep. He'll be relaxing on the couch while I'm scurrying around, stressed out about accomplishing all the many things I've piled up on my plate. In moments like this, I have wished we could change places.

I've been envious, too, of Ossy's ability to trust God to guide him. It seemed like it took me forever to understand my purpose. Not my husband. He would say to me, "The footsteps of a righteous man are ordered of the Lord; if I'm missing it, the Holy Spirit will correct me." So, I would look at him and wish we could just change places for a while.

Every time I entertained thoughts like these, I wasn't walking in love towards my husband. And I was missing out on the blessing our complementary strengths and weaknesses bring to both of us. You see, the parties in a covenant relationship take on the strengths of each other and shore up each other's weaknesses.

When I came to understand this, instead of wanting to change places with him, I've let my husband use his strengths to help me. For instance, when I become overwhelmed with my to-do list, talking to him helps me grow calm. He listens, encourages, and shows me ways to simplify my life-- sometimes by helping me figure out the most important thing I need to focus on at the time. And sometimes by doing some things on my to-do list so I can focus on my priorities. I've come to realize that his life is my life too, so I have reason to be grateful for him rather than jealous.

Now to the other part: the boiling over with jealousy bit. The jealousy referred to here is not the positive aspect of the word, like when Scripture says God is a jealous God, meaning He passionately loves His people. The jealousy referred to here is more of the obsessive, suspicious kind.

Let me give you an example. In my first year of marriage, I was always worried about what girl was calling my husband or sending him text messages. One time, after a female customer of his called him just to say hi, I called her back and told her, "Stop calling my husband"! I shudder now at that level of insecurity.

Now, please don't get me wrong, I am a firm advocate of accountability between partners in marriage. Each person should know what's going on with the other. But love means trusting each other, and when there is trust; jealousy gets the back burner. Trusting each other means we both know we won't entertain anything that would threaten our marriage. As a businessman, my husband's job demands that he interact with women. I should have trusted him to deal with this woman and let her know she was not to call him in the evenings nor on weekends-- or just to say hi.

We wives can also be jealous of the attention our husband gives to other people, including friends and family. We can be jealous of certain activities we believe are taking up the attention meant for us. For instance, I know of wives who resent football. They feel relegated to the background and that the match is more important, and their husbands are having all the fun… jealousy right there. So, what do I do in that case? Rather than boil over when my husband has friends over to watch a game, I prepare popcorn, chill some drinks, serve the guys and use that time to do something else -maybe get my nails done. Why? Because with this attitude, my husband will prefer to stay home and invite the boys over for the game rather than go out to the bar to watch. Better for everyone, right?

Love Is Not Boastful or Vainglorious, Does Not Display Itself Haughtily (V.4)

Loving my husband involves acknowledging that my success is his success. We are a team. I can't be proud and throw my achievements in my man's face, because he always is a contributing factor to my accomplishments.

For instance, I am a writer, and when I complete a book, it's a big deal for me. But to think that it was all me would be a lie. Why? Because if my husband hadn't helped, the book would not have been written. He encouraged me, read and reread my drafts, listened to my ideas (even when they weren't so great), prodded me to act when I was being lazy, ordered takeout food to give me time to write, let me sleep in after long nights on the computer... Get my point? In reality, my success is really our success.

Love means sharing our wins and recognizing that one person's success is the success of the whole team. Thinking like this keeps me from being haughty.

Love Is Not Conceited (V.5)

According to the dictionary, *conceit* is a state of pride arising out of an overestimation of one's own ability, possessions, or importance.[17] There are many ways pride can rear its ugly head in marriage, for instance:

Being too proud to ask for or seek help for instance. Loving my husband means being willing to seek expert help when necessary. It means I won't shy away from seeing a marriage counsellor if necessary.

Thinking more highly of myself than I ought. I'm not against healthy self –esteem; what I'm referring to is a form of self -delusion. I must be able to make and accept an honest assessment of myself. I also need to be able to accept constructive criticism. That way I can improve on any areas of weakness.

For example, until I met my husband, I used to think I made fantastic melon soup. But he didn't like my soup. At first, I resented that. Why couldn't he appreciate my efforts? What was wrong with my version of melon soup? Even if my soup tasted different from the melon soup he was used to, why couldn't he just change his tastes? If you listen closely, you'll hear the shrill voice of PRIDE. And as long as I kept thinking that way, my melon soup was something we quibbled over.

Then I put my feelings aside and decided to figure out if I could make my melon soup better—well, at least for hubby (no one else had complained). So, I googled it, found a recipe with a lot of positive reviews, followed the instructions, and turned out a truly lovely soup. Guess what? The new version was better. Everyone said so, even those who liked my old version. If I hadn't laid down my pride, I would not have been able to improve in this area.

Being selfish or self-centered. For example, pride can make me act like my career or vocation is more important than my responsibilities to my husband. I would selfishly expect my husband to adjust and understand. Pride can cause me to think it's okay to leave my husband to fend for himself. After all, I'm out early, get home late, and I'm tired. Now before the women's liberation hat comes on, hear me out. I'm talking here about an attitude of the heart. Can or should our husbands fix meals sometimes or help around the house? Certainly, but I'm saying that as a wife I shouldn't shirk my responsibilities either.

Not admitting when I'm wrong or saying I'm sorry. Pride makes us think doing so is a sign of weakness. Pride refuses to "lose" an argument or fight. While I must have a healthy regard for who I am, loving my husband means NOT placing myself higher than him in the scale of importance. I'm neither superior nor inferior to him.

Love Is Not Rude and Does Not Act Unbecomingly (V. 5)

This one is straight to the point, isn't it? This reminds me that it's not okay to be Mrs. Polite and Courteous only when I'm in public or with friends and colleagues, only to drop the ball when I'm home.

If I am kind, speak nicely and show courtesy and good manners to those I interact with outside my home, I should treat my husband even more so. What he thinks of me should matter more to me than the opinions of strangers. Sometimes it's easy to take our loved ones for granted, because we know they love us.

So, what does rude look like?

- Interrupting him mid-sentence because I think I have something more important to say or because I'm not interested in what he's saying.

- Changing a TV channel he's watching without asking if it was okay.

- Snapping at him or making sarcastic comments.

- Using him as the butt of coarse jokes.

- Being moody and irritable. (Nope, it's not okay to say it's a woman thing. I'm in control of my emotions, or at least I should be.)

- Raising my voice at him

- Ignoring him.

I could go on and on. Point is, I should never treat my husband in any way that I would consider as being rude from anyone else.

Love Does Not Insist on Its Own Rights … It Is Not Self-Seeking (V.5)

I know my rights, and I'm glad that I have them: the right to my opinion, the right to religious choice, and so on. Not insisting on my own rights doesn't mean I become the underdog and allow my husband to trample over me. In this context it refers to a lack of selfishness.

For instance, I have the right to eat anything I find in my fridge, but when I save something for my husband, like the last piece of cake and not insisting on my right to eat whatever is in my fridge, I am thinking about him and not just myself. That's what it means to love my husband. Love is consciously giving up some of my rights to make his life more comfortable. I have the right to listen to any genre of music, but loving my husband means allowing him to choose the music we listen to on a road trip. It means not insisting we rent a "romcom" instead of an "action flick" on our movie nights. While I have the right to watch any movie I want, because I love my husband, I happily watch his selection. I'm not saying it always has to be about his way, but that I don't mind foregoing certain liberties now and then. The point is, my attitude shouldn't be "it's either my way or no way".

Love Is Not Touchy or Fretful or Resentful; It Takes No Account of the Evil Done to

It (V. 5)

As a relatively new bride, I struggled with this characteristic of love. I watched my husband suspiciously, to be sure I caught any possible faults and nipped them in the bud. If he said or did something I didn't like, I might not complain about it, but inwardly I seethed (and the poor man wouldn't even know what was wrong!).

A few months after I got married, I watched the movie Brothers. In one scene some women are told that it's a sign of true love if your husband gives you the last morsel of food rather than take it himself. So, what did I do? I started setting traps to see if my husband loved me with all his heart. I would serve him some food, then watch to see if he would give me the last bite without my asking for it. If he did offer it to me I would refuse, expecting that he insist I eat it. One day I happened to tell him about this love test and he started laughing. His reaction made me realize how silly it was to think that he didn't love me simply because he didn't always leave me the last bite of food. I also realized that I was subconsciously afraid of not being loved by the man I married. In my bid to protect myself, I became a suspicious, distrustful, touchy, and resentful woman.

Loving my husband means learning to be less defensive and suspicious of his every act. The last part of this verse says, "pay no attention to a suffered wrong". What does this mean? Does it mean I put myself continuously in a position to be hurt or that I let myself be abused? No! Rather, it means that I'm no longer easily offended. My husband doesn't have to walk on eggshells around me, never knowing what might trip me off. It means excusing minor infringements and easily forgiving him for his failures and hurts. It means not throwing his past offenses back in his face or keeping a scorecard.

Love Does Not Rejoice at Injustice and Unrighteousness, But Rejoices When Right and Truth Prevail (V.6)

This verse is about encouraging Ossy to live a life of godliness: it teaches me to discourage and not support sin in my husband's life.

An example of a wife who failed to do that in the Bible is Jezebel and she's become an example of what a wife shouldn't be.

> But there was no one like Ahab who sold himself to do wickedness in the sight of the Lord, because Jezebel his wife stirred him up (1 Kings 21:25).

Scripture says Jezebel stirred Ahab up to do evil, how did she do that? A wife has a lot of influence in her husband's life, Jezebel used her influence to encourage Ahab to sin rather than steer him away from evil. She not only encouraged him but helped perpetuate evil. An example is when she got him Naboth's vineyard:

Naboth Is Murdered for His Vineyard (1 Kings 21:1-25)

And it came to pass after these things that Naboth the Jezreelite had a vineyard which was in Jezreel, next to the palace of Ahab king of Samaria. ² So Ahab spoke to Naboth, saying, "Give me your vineyard, that I may have it for a vegetable garden, because it is near, next to my house; and for it I will give you a vineyard better than it. Or, if it seems good to you, I will give you its worth in money."

³ But Naboth said to Ahab, "The Lord forbid that I should give the inheritance of my fathers to you!"

⁴ So Ahab went into his house sullen and displeased because of the word which Naboth the Jezreelite had spoken to him; for he had said, "I will not give you the inheritance of my fathers." And he lay down on his bed, and turned away his face, and would eat no food. ⁵ But Jezebel his wife came to him, and said to him, "Why is your spirit so sullen that you eat no food?"

⁶ He said to her, "Because I spoke to Naboth the Jezreelite, and said to him, 'Give me your vineyard for money; or else, if it pleases you, I will give you another vineyard for it.' And he answered, 'I will not give you my vineyard.'"

⁷ Then Jezebel his wife said to him, "You now exercise authority over Israel! Arise, eat food, and let your heart be cheerful; I will give you the vineyard of Naboth the Jezreelite."

⁸ And she wrote letters in Ahab's name, sealed them with his seal, and sent the letters to the elders and the nobles who were dwelling in the city with Naboth. ⁹ She wrote in the letters, saying,

Proclaim a fast, and seat Naboth [a] with high honour among the people; ¹⁰ and seat two men, scoundrels, before him to bear witness against him, saying, "You have blasphemed God and the king." Then take him out, and stone him, that he may die.

¹¹ So the men of his city, the elders and nobles who were inhabitants of his city, did as Jezebel had sent to them, as it was written in the letters which she had sent to them. ¹² They proclaimed a fast, and seated Naboth with high honour among the people. ¹³ And two men, scoundrels, came in and sat before him; and the scoundrels witnessed against him, against Naboth, in the presence of the people, saying, "Naboth has blasphemed God and the king!" Then they took him outside the city and stoned him with stones, so that he died. 14 Then they sent to Jezebel, saying, "Naboth has been stoned and is dead."

¹⁵ And it came to pass, when Jezebel heard that Naboth had been stoned and was dead, that Jezebel said to Ahab, "Arise, take possession of the vineyard of Naboth the Jezreelite, which he refused to give you for money; for Naboth is not alive, but dead." [16] *So it was, when Ahab heard that Naboth was dead, that Ahab got up and went down to take possession of the vineyard of Naboth the Jezreelite.*

Jezebel not only encouraged Ahab's covetousness but engineered the plot to dispossess Naboth of his possession and even had him killed!

Because I love my husband, I commit to be a source of godly advice and support. Whenever, we have a decision to make I will always support 'what is right'. A lot of the wrong in society could be changed if the significant others stop welcoming the spoils of unrighteousness.

Love Never Fails (V. 8)

This last verse summarizes everything I've said so far. Amazing stuff! If my love for my husband - and his love for me -contains the characteristics of love outlined in 1 Corinthians 13, the likelihood of our marriage getting into trouble become really, really slim.

Now, if you're anything like me, you may be tempted roll your eyes at this description of love and think, *That's impossible!* . And you'd be right to think so, right in the sense that on our own we cannot love anyone like that. But the good news is that when we have Christ in us, we have the ability love in this way, *for the love of God is shed abroad in our hearts by the Holy Spirit (Romans 5:5).*

Love never fails... because marriage is the responsibility of two- the man and his wife-, this verse is only true as relating to the marriage relationship when both parties love the way God prescribes.

I cannot force my husband to love me this way, but if I love him just like the Bible asks me to, then the chances of him responding to my love positively and learning to love me the same way become higher.

My job is to do my bit in making my marriage work, so I've decided to love Ossy God's way—which is why I read 1 Corinthians 13 at least once a month. I recommend you do the same as a way of checking your love meter.

Chef Tips

✓ Read 1 Corinthians 13 and do a self-check.

✓ Make a commitment to love your husband God's way.

✓ Ask God for forgiveness for where you've missed it and for help to love your husband with a 1 Corinthians 13 kind of love.

The Marriage Recipe

Ingredients:

+God
+Love

+Honour
+Lovemaking
+Commitment

III

Honour

Take delight in honouring each other. (Romans 12:10 NLT)

I love ice-cream! One of my earliest memories is of my dad taking me to an ice-cream shop for the first time. To my five-year-old eyes, the array of beautifully coloured ice-cream lining the walls was one of the best things I had seen. I remember pressing my nose against the glass and not knowing which flavour to choose from the myriad of options before me. But then my father said it was okay to have as many flavours as I wanted and that I could always come back for more. From that first taste I was hooked...

As an adult, I've learnt that the recipe for ice-cream includes an emulsifier: something that makes those difficult to mix ingredients (like oil and water) combine well together and stops them from separating out. That's what ingredients like eggs and milk do in ice-cream. Besides, creating a workable mix and a smoother texture, the emulsifier/s also gives the ice-cream stability: they stop the ice-cream from melting rapidly after serving.

In our marriage recipe, honour acts like our emulsifier- honour helps Ossy and I work well together, improves the quality of our marriage and makes it more stable.

According to my thesaurus, *honour* has these synonyms: "esteem, respect, admire, value, cherish, defer to." [18] The Greek word for honour- timao, means "to prize, i.e. fix a valuation upon; by implication, to revere".[19] Showing honour, then, means treating someone respectfully because you value that person.

Honouring my husband is not an emotional response and is not based on his behaviour- I choose to honour him whether he deserves it or not- Honouring Ossy is my decision to view him as a priceless treasure, as a person of high worth and value: it is my gift to him.

But why should I honour my husband? Because:

i.   God commands it.:

> *However, each man among you [without exception] is to love his wife as his very own self [with behaviour worthy of respect and esteem, always seeking the best for her with an attitude of lovingkindness], <u>and the wife [must see to it] that she respects and delights in her husband [that she notices him and prefers him and treats him with loving concern, treasuring him, honouring him, and holding him dear].</u>* *(Ephesians 5:33 Amp)*

Remember our first ingredient- putting God into my marriage by obeying His principles? Honouring Ossy is part of me doing that.

ii.   My husband is valuable- lots of scripture tell me this:

- He's created in God's image

> *So, God created man in His own image; in the image of God He created him; male and female He created them. (Genesis 1:27).*

When God created man, He used the best prototype possible- Himself. That's how valuable man is to Him. Why shouldn't I value one made after the likeness of God?

- God Himself places so much value on His creation. In Job 7:17, the writer marvels at just how much value God has placed on man.

What is man that You should magnify him and think him important? And that You are concerned about him? (AMP)

If God thinks my husband is important it makes sense that I should too, right?

iii. So that my prayers won't be hindered.

The last part of 1 Peter 3:7 though talking to husbands with regards to their wives reads:

…show her honour and respect as a fellow heir of the grace of life, so that your prayers will not be hindered or ineffective (AMP)

I know this scripture was addressed to men, but God isn't gender biased. If not honouring me can hinder my husband's prayers I'm pretty sure not honouring Ossy would do the same for me. Remember according to that verse he's a fellow heir of the grace of life.

So how do I honour my husband?

By Thinking Well of Him

I can only be a wife who honours her husband if my thoughts about/towards him are honourable. Why? Because what I think of him will influence how I relate to him; it will influence my words, my actions, my attitude, and my response toward him. Knowing that, I keep to Paul's admonition to think good, wholesome thoughts about my husband.

Finally, brethren, whatsoever things are true, whatsoever things are honest, whatsoever things are just, whatsoever things are pure, whatsoever things are of good report; if there be any virtue, if there be any praise, think on these things. (Philippians 4:8 NKJV)

This verse gives me the criteria for the kind of thoughts I should entertain about my husband; they must be honest, just, pure, and of a good report. I'm to think of his virtues and those things for which I can praise him for. I'm to focus on the positives. Why? Because when I focus on the negative, it blinds me to all the great things about him. The negative gets magnified and becomes all I can see. But when I focus on the positive, and think of my husband as a king, it makes it easy to treat him as one.

Is it easy to always think honourably about him? Of course not. It's something I must keep checking up on, because dishonourable thoughts are not always obvious and can sometimes seem innocent.

For example, years ago, I thought I was the more spiritual partner. I believed I prayed more (and better) and spent more time in Christian activities (Bible study, church meetings and so on). As a result, I more or less hijacked our devotion and study times and tried to handle spiritual matters by myself. But those thoughts were putting me at variance with God's order of things. When I realized this and stopped feeling superior to my husband, my eyes opened to the fact that he was a strong believer and that by partnering with him, I could better achieve God's purposes.

Truth be told, I now believe that my dishonourable thoughts were a hindrance to my husband's spiritual expression. Once I stopped thinking he couldn't pray as well, his prayers became power-packed and result producing! No, I suddenly didn't become deluded; I just stopped being full of pride in that area and stopped subtly criticizing him- I stopped making comments like 'you forgot to pray about this or that' or 'you should have used this scripture or that scripture to pray'. So, by stepping out of his way, I gave my husband room to grow and to be the spiritual head of our home.

By Being Faithful

My marriage bed must be undefiled.

> *Marriage is to be held in honor among all [that is, regarded as something of great value], and the marriage bed undefiled [by immorality or by any sexual sin]; for God will judge the sexually immoral and adulterous. (Heb.13:4 AMP)*

My body belongs to my husband only, and I'm responsible for ensuring there's no trespassing, virtual or otherwise. So, no cheating of any kind, and that includes secret, sexual fantasies about other people, real or imagined. No suggestive conversations or flirtations.

Being faithful to my husband also means that he is the only person for whom I try to be or look sexy. I know that's a hard pill to swallow, especially since society tells us that part of being a successful woman is being sexy. I'm not saying we shouldn't try to be attractive but being attractive is not the same thing as being sexy. *Sexy* is synonymous with *seductive, inviting, sensual, provocative,* and *tempting*[20] In other words, being sexy is to act and or dress in such a way as to make someone feel sexually attracted to you.

The only person a wife should want to attract sexually is her husband. And with that understanding, some fashion trends are a no-no. Being faithful in marriage means covering up. I certainly don't want some stranger staring down my décolleté or catching glimpses of my "cheeks" or inner thighs. You get my drift. God expects me to live a chaste life before my husband.

By Serving Him

To serve is to attend to or wait upon. To understand what it means to serve your husband, let me ask you a question. Would you agree that how your server attends to you at a restaurant influences your opinion of the place and the size of your tip? It certainly influences me!

The server is no way inferior to me when she waits on me because it's her job but because I am paying for the service, I have certain expectations. Picture this. I walk into a café, sit down, and it takes ten minutes to get the server's attention. When she finally gets to me, she's distracted. I place my order and when I ask how long it will take to get my food, she says fifteen minutes. I wait for forty-five minutes-- and still no food. Just when I'm about to leave, the server brings my order; she offers me no apologies or explanations. Besides that, she has also mixed up my order, so I didn't even get what I had asked for. Would you say I was well-served? Of course not! The reason for that illustration? To show the difference service or a lack of it can make.

The same analogy can apply to marriage. Marriage involves doing things for my loved one. Serving my husband means waiting on him. It means that I cook, clean, and pick up after him. It means I wash, dry, iron, and fold his laundry. It's doing what I can to make his life easier. Now don't get me wrong. I'm not saying that I personally do all the cleaning, cooking, and household chores. I get help when I can. I take shirts to the drycleaner down the road, occasionally hire a housecleaning service or order take-out food. But my attitude toward my husband is, what can I do to make your life better today?

Before you crucify me for saying a wife should serve her husband, let me remind you of what Jesus did: He washed His disciples' feet (John 13:1-17). It's easy to miss what a big deal this was. You see, in biblical times it was the job of a servant to wash the feet of his master and/or guests. Not the other way around. And just think about how dirty those feet must have been--encrusted with desert dust. But Jesus washed off the dirt and grime anyway. (If you have ever had a pedicure, you know how good it feels to have someone clean your feet.). Why did He wash the disciple's feet? Because He was setting an example. He was saying, be a servant to each other.

Here's what I'm saying. I cannot get away from doing acts of kindness for my husband if I'm to have a blissful marriage. (Remember this book is for women, so I am focusing on what wives should do. In marriage, a couple should serve each other. There's nothing wrong with husbands helping out around the house!).

Through My Communication With Him

There's no way two people can interact without communication. That's why this is one very key aspect of relating with my husband. Communication involves sending and receiving information (whether verbally or non-verbally -more on that later). Relating with my husband involves sharing my thoughts, feelings, ideas, sharing pertinent information about myself, the world around and anything that affects or involves us with him. It also includes my ability to listen, understand and respond to him as he expresses his thoughts, emotions etc.

When messages are sent, understood, and responded to, then communication has happened. So, in marriage communication looks like this

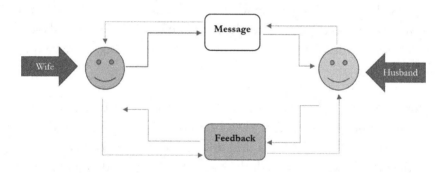

In other words:

communication = clear message + listening + feedback

So, using this model how do I ensure that through my communication I am honouring my husband?

First, through my message (I'll be using the term 'message' to refer to both my originating messages and the feedback/responses I give my husband).

Quick note here- messages can be either verbal or non-verbal; by verbal messages I mean language-based ones: spoken, written, text, print…, non-verbal messages on the other hand are those related to my body language and other little nuances of behavior- these include my tone and pitch of voice, facial expressions, gestures etc.

So how do I ensure that my messages honour my husband? I use the following guidelines, my messages:

¶¶ Are clear

There are a lot of messages I want to send to my husband: I love you, I'm upset, I need something, let's do something or go somewhere together, and so on. To communicate those messages successfully, I must make the message clear and simple (it's easy to complicate my message, so this can sometimes be a challenge!). I must learn to say or show what I mean and not leave it to inference or guesswork.

For instance, when what I want to know is if my husband can tell I've lost some weight, I ask him, "Can you tell I lost some weight?" instead of something vague, like "How do I look?" Because my husband (like most men) tends to communicate literally, "How do I look?" means just that. So, he'll probably respond with "nice" or "okay"—and I'll think he said that I'm fat. But he didn't…

So, if I don't want my messages to get lost in transmission, I really must say what I mean.

¶¶ Are responses (where applicable) based on what was said and not my suspicions, interpretations or inferences.

The first year I was married, I tended to 'hear' more than what was said and 'discern' hidden meanings from the messages I got from my husband and it caused a communication breakdown.

For instance, if my husband came home and said something like, "This room needs sweeping", what I would hear was, "You really need to improve on your housekeeping". But guess what? That was the voice in my head, my own insecurity talking. My husband was simply stating a fact and would usually get out the broom and sweep the room himself. He wasn't trying to imply that I wasn't keeping a clean house.

So now I've learnt to deal with any areas of insecurity and to ask for clarification when I'm unsure of what Ossy is trying to tell me.

¶¶ Are wholesome and build Ossy up not tear him down.

> *"Do not let unwholesome [foul, profane, worthless, vulgar] words ever come out of your mouth, but only such speech as is good for building up others, according to the need and the occasion, so that it will be a blessing to those who hear [you speak]." Eph. 4:29*

That means I have no excuse to be sarcastic, swear at him, use vile words, verbally bash him or criticize him. Funny that word 'criticize'- in the past I used to think it was okay to offer some 'constructive criticism'. Problem with that is that the words criticism and criticize are not positive ones. According to the dictionary[21], to criticize is to indicate the faults of (someone or something) in a disapproving way. Its synonyms include attack, disparage, malign, denounce, vilify… none of these words connote anything I should be doing to my husband. So, no criticisms- no matter how well intentioned.

Besides ensuring that the words I speak to my husband are wholesome and encourage him, I also watch that my non -verbal cues are also good ones. No hissing or other sounds of contempt, no derogatory eye rolls or looks, no smirks or scowls, no stances of defiance (hands akimbo etc.), no to a raised voice, no rude or angry tones…

Honouring Ossy also means that I'm quick to praise him, I affirm him. I tell him how special and wonderful he is! I magnify every good quality no matter how little. I endeavor to make him feel like the king he is! I use my words, gestures and everything else to communicate to my husband that he is the most important person in my life!

I'm quick to express gratitude too. I say thank you for everything, even for loving me. I don't take him for granted and make sure that he knows that I value him and everything he does for me and our family. I send him lovely text messages, hide love notes in his wallet and pockets, surprise him with gifts and give him a massage every now and then. The reason for all this? To communicate unequivocally to Ossy that I honour him.

🍴 Support peace

I want my home to be peaceful, one way I ensure that is by endeavouring to keep strife out the door. How?

> - I avoid fighting and quarrelling: this is not the same as avoiding conflicts because conflicts are an inevitable consequence of relating with one another (more on conflict resolution in a bit). When we have disagreements, I choose not to fight or let it degenerate into quarrelling. I also diffuse volatile situations as quickly as I can- I speak softly, avoid aggressive body language, use silence or walk away (when that won't worsen things). It might seem like backing down from a fight is a sign of weakness but that's far from the truth. It is actually harder to backdown from a fight than it is to jump right in. So why back down? Because scripture teaches me that it is the wise thing to do-

> *Avoiding a fight is a mark of honor; only fools insist on quarreling. Prov. 20:3 (NLT)*

> *A gentle answer deflects anger, but harsh words make tempers flare. Prov. 15:1(NLT)*

> *A fool gives vent to all his feelings, but the wise, thinking of afterwards, stills them (CJB)*

> - I avoid nagging

Nagging, in interpersonal communication, is repetitive behaviour in the form of pestering, hectoring, or otherwise continuously urging an individual to complete previously discussed requests or act on advice.[22]

Okay, I would never want to be a nagging wife but sometimes I do get carried away with the urge to give Ossy 'reminders'. Now there's nothing wrong with a reminder every now and then, but when it becomes continuous I need to put myself in check. So, for example if we need some plumbing work done and hubby has agreed to call the plumber, after about two reminders I'll get an alternative solution – I'll either set a reminder on his phone or better yet call the plumber myself. That's better than nagging him to do it- 'have you called the plumber yet?', 'when are you going to call the plumber?' 'Why haven't you called the plumber?', 'We really need to get this leak fixed and you still haven't called the plumber'... I'm tired myself after reading that and feel like screaming 'just go ahead and call the plumber yourself! The point is, no one likes being nagged, husbands inclusive. The Bible describes it like this:

> *It's better to stay outside on the roof of your house than to live inside with a nagging wife. Prov. 21:9(CEV)*

Okay so I want Ossy in the house, so NO to nagging!

▌▐ Are what I intended to send in the first place

This involves checking up on unintentional messages. Let me explain. Sometime ago, the stone on my engagement ring fell out, so I took it off with plans to get the stone replaced. Sometime later I bought a ring I called my Jesus ring, because it has little crosses engraved all around. To me the ring was a symbol of my devotion to Christ. Since I hadn't yet replaced the stone on my engagement ring, I wore my Jesus ring next to my wedding band. Every now and then, my husband would make comments like, "I see you no longer like your engagement ring" or, 'Why do you have that ring on your wedding ring finger?" I would laugh and say, "Oh, as soon as I get the engagement ring fixed, I'll put it back on."

I was washing my hands one day and the Holy Spirit opened my eyes to the reality of what my actions were communicating to my husband. Here's the message I was sending: I no longer valued the ring he had given me - I'd worn it consistently for over a decade, but when I lost the stone, I displayed no urgency in getting it replaced. This message was causing my husband to wonder if my love for him was diminishing as well.

I realized that I'd been sending a message that I had never intended to send—and an awful one at that! The thing is, I would never want my husband to believe that I didn't place the highest value on the ring he had given me—or that my love for him had waned. I told him how sorry I was for making him think I preferred my Jesus ring to my engagement ring and promised to never put any ring he didn't buy for me on my ring finger. I started wearing my Jesus ring on another finger and made enquiries about replacing my lost stone. Turns out I was able to do so in less than a month. You should have seen the smile on my husband's face as he put my engagement ring back on my finger.

The last part of communication to be discussed here is listening and listening affects my feedback or responses.

To listen is 'to hear what someone has said and understand that it is serious, important, or true.'[23]

Why did I say 'listening affects my responses'? Because it is what I heard that would determine what I say or do in reply.

So, listening is really important. I've found though that if I don't make conscious effort, I might think I'm listening to Ossy when I'm not. And what causes the breakdown in listening for me?

Distractions - I used to think I was expected to be great at multitasking until I read somewhere that the brain can only consciously do one thing at a time and that when I think I'm multi-tasking, I'm really just mentally jumping from one task to another much like a juggler. Not only that, I learnt that by continually shifting from one task to another I never really give my best to either one. So, I've thrown out that proverbial picture: - you know, the one with the woman with a phone on one ear, baby in one arm, the other arm stirring a pot on the stove and her ironing on the table behind her! I could never keep up anyway 😊! What's the point of this? When I'm listening to Ossy, I'm focused on doing that and not 101 other little things at the same time. When I can, I give him a 100% attention when he's speaking. So, if I'm in the middle of my favorite TV show for instance, I hit the pause on Gibbs[24], so I can listen or if I'm in the middle of an intense novel, I place a bookmark in, drop the book and pay attention. Sometimes though, the distractions are not physical things- rather my thoughts wandering this way and that. In that case, once I catch myself drifting, I refocus and if I've missed anything, apologize and ask Ossy to repeat what was said.

Haste- When I'm in a hurry to respond without listening to the end or when I'm rushing off to do something else, I can miss out on what my husband is saying. Listening, involves patience, it implies taking the time to make sure I got the right message, understood it, before I think of responding or acting. Scripture says;

> .... *a person in a hurry makes mistakes. Prov. 19:2(GW)*

AND

> *Understand this, my beloved brothers and sisters. Let everyone be quick to hear [be a careful, thoughtful listener], slow to speak [a speaker of carefully chosen words and], slow to anger [patient, reflective, forgiving]; James 1:9 (AMP)*

Rehearsing my response- If I'm busy planning what to say next, I miss out on chunks of what my husband is saying. Not only that but doing so makes me discourteous because if I'm rehearsing my next speech then I'm going to be interrupting him every now and then, just so I can have my say- and that's never a good way to communicate.

> *A fool finds no satisfaction in trying to understand, for he would rather express his own opinion. Prov. 18:2 (ISV)*

Ouch! But God's always right. So, while it's good to express my opinion, it's also important that I also seek to understand Ossy's messages to me.

The last thing I want to discuss under communicating with my husband is how I resolve conflict:

I said earlier that conflicts are inevitable, that's because Ossy and I are two separate individuals and as we continually relate with each other we will sometimes misunderstand each other, say or do the wrong things or just miss the mark with each other. How we deal with those moments contribute to how successful our marriage is. Here, I'll be sharing what I do to resolve conflict in my home:

- I start with the mindset that Ossy is not my enemy and that having a disagreement at the time doesn't shake my love for him. So, throughout the process I am kind, patient, respectful and forgiving. Conflicts are not battles I must win at all costs, I always think win-win. Again, my husband is not my enemy- we're on the same side.

- I don't try to resolve our arguments when either of us is still in the heat of our emotions. I let us both calm down/cool off and then we can talk about our differences.

- I never let our conflicts linger, I never go to bed angry with my husband- even if it takes till the wee hours of the morning to finally smooth things over. My motto about this is culled from scripture 'when angry, do not sin: do not ever let your wrath (your exasperation, your fury or indignation) last until the sun goes down'- Ephesians 4:26 (AMPC)

- I listen to Ossy's point of view without being defensive or critical.

- I take responsibility for my part in the conflict- *how did I contribute to the conflict? What should/could I have done differently?*

- I seek to make peace- I apologize where I'm wrong and forgive where I've been offended.

Let me give a practical example; one time, after a long afternoon at the mall, Ossy and I decided to have a quick lunch at one of the in-house eateries. The problem was that by the time we got to the ground floor, it seemed like every food spot was teaming with people and I wanted to eat somewhere with a little more privacy. By the time we tried the fourth food court, Ossy had enough- we could either get food there or not at all and I didn't think he was particularly gracious about it. So, I got upset too.

At this point, both of us were tired, hungry and upset at each other- Ossy because he felt I was too picky and me because I felt he should have been more understanding. So, what did I do?

First, I reigned in my initial impulse to tell him how I felt about his reaction. Why? Because talking about it then would have only escalated things- none of us could communicate effectively at that point.

Next, I ordered food and sat with him to eat- and avoided looking angry or ignoring him. After lunch, we left the shops and headed home. Again, I resisted the temptation to start airing my grievances – it was neither the time nor the place.

By the time we got home, we were both calmer and we could talk. It was now easier to tell him without raising my voice or being aggressive that I didn't like the way he'd spoken to me earlier. I was also calm enough to listen to him explain that I had made too much of a fuss about there being too many people at the food court.

Now I could see why he felt that way. Did that excuse his snapping at me? Certainly not, but I could understand why he did and was able to forgive him. I could also see that I had indeed been too picky, so it was easy to apologize.

The beauty of handling it this way is that Ossy apologized. He'd also had time to mull things over and realized he shouldn't have snapped and could have been a little more accommodating.

The point is that if I'd let my emotions rule, we would have had a full-blown quarrel on our hands. Now this might seem like a minor one on the scale of possible conflicts, but the same principles apply.

By Showing Regard

Still another way I honour my husband is in how I treat or show regard for his person and the things related to him. I speak well of him when we are together in public and when he is not present. While my hubby is a terrific person, he is not perfect (nobody is). Even so, his little flaws are not morsels for discussion--with anyone. It's my job to magnify the good in my spouse. I don't disparage him; I tell of his many good points, and I'm quick to defend him.

This is so important. I've seen women insult their husbands repeatedly, telling everyone "he's irresponsible", "good for nothing", and the like. Then they are shocked when someone else treats their man disrespectfully. Really? After they've just been talking about what a difficult man he is? What do these wives expect? (Quick point here. I'm not against speaking to Christian counsellors with the aim of working on a troubled marriage. What I'm saying is that it can be harmful to your marriage relationship if you speak badly of your husband to third parties.)

Showing regard for my husband means that I respect the people and interests that concern him. So, for instance, I give him space when he needs to concentrate on work--; that's not the time to interrupt him for issues that can wait till later. I also show him respect by how I treat his family, friends, colleagues and those he relates with. I treat them with kindness and welcome them into our home. I give him space to hang out with the boys too.

I also show regard for his stuff. I handle his belongings with care and put them away nicely. I don't throw them out or give them away without his permission, even if they're old or he hasn't used them in a while.

By Submitting to Him

I used to defend gender equality and resisted any implication that I was less than any man. Just the word *submission* would make me angry, in part because I'd met a few overzealous men who believed that this word means subjugation and a loss of identity and that just because I was a woman, I was somehow less than a man or second-class.

I had a bone to pick with God too. I didn't choose to be female, so why would He create me to be a woman, and then make me less?

But my view changed when I saw for myself that God never said that a woman is "less" than a man. He never said that women are not equal to men or that we are subject to men just because we are women.

Although I still believe that men and women are created equal (and Scripture backs this), *'Faith in Christ Jesus is what makes each of you equal with each other, whether you are a Jew or a Greek, a slave or a free person, a man or a woman.'* Gal. 3:28 CEV

I also believe in the biblical model of gender-based role assignments within marriage. The Bible teaches us that the husband is the head of his wife (Ephesians 5: 23). This is God's organogram for marriage, and the foundation of the concept of submission.

Think of it this way. All organizations have an organizational chart that defines reporting lines-- trainee reporting to supervisor; supervisor reporting to manager; manager reporting to GM, and so forth. This hierarchy creates order and allows a smooth flow of operations. There can only be one boss.

Submitting to my supervisors at work, most of whom were men, was never a problem for me. The reason had nothing to do with gender; it had everything to do with my designation. Because I respected the rules of the organizations I worked for (and wanted to keep my job), I worked well with my bosses. I learned to work with their personalities and work/ leadership styles, and made sure our goals were met. I wasn't rude to my boss; I didn't yell at him; I didn't refuse to follow his directives or usurp his authority. When irreconcilable differences arose, I knew to escalate my case to someone higher up the chain of command or to HR.

Funny how it's often easy to submit within the context of work or career, but a struggle when it is "thus sayeth the Lord" and in a marriage.

According to Ephesians 5:22-23, God's marriage organogram looks like this:

Wife reporting to husband > Husband reporting to God

Put another way, the husband is the pilot, the wife is the co-pilot, and they both report to air traffic control: God. Would you want to be on a flight where the co-pilot disregarded the chain of command? I wouldn't either. When I saw that submission is about following a chain of command in marriage, my attitude changed.

First Peter 3: 1 says:

> *In the same way, you wives, be [a]submissive to your own husbands [subordinate, not as inferior, but out of respect for the responsibilities entrusted to husbands and their accountability to God, and so partnering with them] so that even if some do not obey the word [of God], they may be won over [to Christ] without discussion by the godly lives of their wives. (AMP)*

I like that rendering of 1 Peter 3:1. I am subordinate, not because I'm inferior, but because I respect my husband's God-given role.

> *Wives, be subject [d]to your own husbands, as [a service] to the Lord. For the husband is head of the wife, as Christ is head of the church, Himself being the Savior of the body. But as the church is subject to Christ, so also wives should be subject to their husbands in everything [respecting both their*

position as protector and their responsibility to God as head of the house]. Ephesians 5:22-24 (AMP)

So, what does submission look like?

In like manner, you married women, be submissive to your own husbands [subordinate yourselves as being secondary to and <u>dependent</u> on them, and <u>adapt</u> yourselves to them], so that even if any do not obey the Word [of God], they may be won over not by discussion but by the [godly] lives of their wives,

When they observe the pure and modest way in which you conduct yourselves, together with your [a]reverence [for your husband; you are to feel for him all that reverence includes: to respect, <u>defer to</u>, revere him—to honor, esteem, appreciate, prize, and, in the human sense, to adore him, that is, to admire, praise, be devoted to, deeply love, and enjoy your husband].(1 Peter 3:1-2, underlining mine).

Please note the underlined words. That's where I get my cue on what submission looks like practically.

Submission implies being dependent on my husband, meaning -- that I rely on him for support. That I acknowledge our connectivity and therefore do not do anything apart from him. Dependency in this sense is not a clinginess or inability to take care of myself or to take necessary actions. It's the understanding that I don't take action without my husband's consent or go-ahead, especially when it comes to major decisions. For instance, I shouldn't shave off all my hair without first convincing my husband that he would like the new, bald me ☺. Seriously though, a husband should have a say-so when it comes to his wife making major decisions like taking a job out of town or changing careers.

Submission also implies that I adapt to my husband. The word adapt is synonymous with words like adjust, acclimatize, accommodate, conform. Yep, it's my job to do the changing. That's sometimes a hard pill to swallow, but it's right there in the Bible. To adapt to my husband, I must get to know him and learn to work and live with his unique personality. I must learn his preferences and accommodate them or conform to them. For example, I love spices in my stew; so, if you let me, I would just about put every spice in: ginger, turmeric, curry, thyme... My husband, on the other hand, doesn't like spicy food. I can either insist on making stews using all my favourite spices, only to have him complain or not eat (which makes us both cranky and feeling unhappy) OR, I can make the stew, take out some for my hubby before I add in the spices I like (or I can skip using the spices all together) –and we're both happy. That's a way of honouring my husband. I am saying to him, "You are valuable to me, so valuable that I am willing to learn what makes you happy and do those things to keep you happy."

So, I have adapted to his preferences and have learned cook our meals his way. And when I'm cooking only for myself, I still go crazy on the spicing. I've adapted in other ways as well- dressing for instance. If you let me, I'll live every day in jeans and sneakers but Ossy likes to see my legs. So, my wardrobe contains skirts and dresses too.

By making these changes in how I do things, I'm not losing my individuality, I am accepting my husband's differences and making the necessary modifications so that we live amicably.

Lastly, submitting to my husband involves *deferring* to him. To defer is to "let another person decide or to accept another person's opinion"[25]. Doing that can be hard, but remember, I must do it God's way or no way. It's easy to agree when my husband I both want the same thing or have the same opinion. But when there're differing views, it's my responsibility to fold (I know... doesn't seem fair right? But God is always just, so my bit is to obey Him, and then let God do the rest).

For example, there've been times when my husband wanted us to make some investment or the other that I didn't agree with. I either wasn't comfortable with the risk involved or would rather we invest in something else, but he insisted. Submitting to him meant that I stopped arguing and trying to push my point. That I let him know that I was willing to follow his lead. I did that and escalated my case to God. What do I mean? I stopped fighting my husband about it and went to God instead about it.

God put my husband in charge, so if anyone can make him change his mind, it would be his "Boss", God.

Funny thing is, most of the time, when I've done that, I begin to see where I was wrong. Sometimes it's in my approach to his suggestions or ideas, other times it's just me being afraid of the unknown (and getting more knowledge helps me get rid of that). And then there've been times when after I'd backed off (and gone to a higher authority ☺), my husband has come back with a change of mind.

My point is this: submission is all about working within the established lines of authority and trusting God that His chain of command works.

I must add a quick note here: submission doesn't mean that I obey my husband at the expense of God's Word. Remember both of us must submit to God. Even if my "boss" asks me to, I am not to break company rules. I am to keep God's Word.

Submission is really a heart attitude: it says I honour your position over me and I'm willing to be led by you. Ultimately, submission should be to God. So as long as submitting to my husband doesn't contradict God's Word I'm in the right place.

By Being Truthful

One very important foundation of a healthy marriage is truth- the absence of lies and falsehood. The dictionary defines truth as 'sincerity in action, character, and utterance[26]. In practical terms, being a wife who is truthful implies that Ossy can be sure that I will always tell him the truth and that He can count on me being true to my word even when it hurts.

> Proverbs says *'The Lord detests lying lips, but He delights in people who are trustworthy"- Proverbs 12:22 (NIV)*

Believe me it's not only God who prefers a person who is trustworthy, I do too. I wouldn't trust someone whose words I couldn't trust. Neither would my husband. So, I have to be someone he can always count on not to lie- not even the 'white ones'. Really though, there really is no such thing as a white lie, a lie is a lie.

By Honouring Myself

It might seem strange to add that I honour my husband by honouring myself, but it is true. Because Ossy is such a treasure to me, I want him to have the best of everything and that includes having the best 'me'. As his wife, I want to be a person of inestimable value- someone important and worth having. Someone who adds value to our relationship rather than detracts from it.

How can I be that? By taking heed to myself and keeping myself valuable. There's a cliché that says *"you can't give what you don't have"*. It applies here, I cannot give Ossy honour when I have none for myself.

So how do I honour myself?

¶ I Stay Spiritually Healthy

To be spiritually healthy, my walk with God must be vibrant. This is the most important way I can take care of myself, because my spiritual health affects every other aspect of who I am. It's impossible to succeed at anything long-term without God's help. On my own and without burning out, I can't do the kinds of things I have talked about in this book. I need His grace to be all He's made me to be and to do all He wants me to do, including being the right kind of wife to my husband. But by staying connected to God, I get the help I need to keep going.

I've found that when I'm spending time with God in prayer, study and worship and going through my day conscious of His presence, I am more productive- I'm better at everything; I'm more patient, less cranky, more efficient, more energetic….

So, I do not neglect fellowship with God and His Word; I remember to read and study the Bible, pray, go to church, read inspirational materials, make faith confessions, and so on etc.

In doing all of that, I remember that it's not the religiosity of the actions that matter, but the substance. That's to say, it's not about reading the Bible so that I can scratch it off my to-do list. It's about reading the Bible knowing its God's love letter to me and wanting to hear from Him daily and to talk to Him daily. It's about going to church so I can be taught from the Word of God and so I can be around people of like faith.

¶¶ I Protect My Mental Health

I stay positive. I avoid worry, anxiety and stress. I exercise my mind. I read, learn new things, and endeavor to keep my mind focused as God advised: on *"whatsoever things are pure and of a good report"* (Phil 4:8). That means that I carefully consider what material I read, watch or listen to because I know it's important that I guard my heart- for what's in my heart determines my life.

> *More than anything you guard, protect your mind, for life flows from it. Prov. 4:23(CEB)*

So, for me it's NO to horror, foul/strong language, violence, pornography and anything that is antichrist or that doesn't glorify God. Sometimes, that might seem like being a bit too extreme but when I remember that the quality of my life and this includes my marriage depends on the state of my mind, shutting those stuff out becomes easier. For example, I tend to get really frightened by scary scenes in movies- even the music can creep me out. What's worse is that even if I manage to sit (with eyes mostly covered and nails digging into Ossy's arm) through the movie I can't shake the fear and images for several nights. I'll have repeated nightmares, lose sleep and become a fearful and cranky Mfon-not really a version of myself that my husband would enjoy. Okay, so maybe I'm just really a scaredy-cat, but even if I wasn't, what benefit does a movie where everyone dies in some gruesome way or where they're tormented by evil forces give me? Even for entertainment, I would rather see something pleasant.

But besides my personal preferences, there's one guiding principle I use in choosing what goes into my mind. I ask myself- *is the content pro God or pro Satan.* So, whenever the underlying theme of any material glorifies the devil, it becomes something I keep OUT.

I find times to relax too. Rest is good. It gives me a chance to reboot and start again renewed and refocused. A refreshed 'me' definitely makes Ossy a better wife because when I'm tired or stressed, I become impatient, irritable, touchy and all the other things that would make hanging out with me less than enjoyable. And relaxing doesn't have to be complicated. Sometimes all that means is taking a nap. It could be listening to some soft music, taking a walk or just closing my eyes for a few minutes. Beyond that, I plan vacations into our family time, so we all get a chance to unwind.

Part of taking care of my mental health includes taking care of my intellect too. I want to keep improving my mind and my awareness of the world around me, so I am continually learning and growing, pushing my limits, challenging myself. I read, read, read. I attend classes and seminars, take courses. I listen to experts; I ask questions; I stretch to become more. That way, I bring more to the table because I become more knowledgeable.

I also specifically read up or listen to materials on issues that interest my husband. That way I can contribute meaningfully to discussions on them and be a good source of counsel whenever he needs it- I cannot give advice on something I know nothing about.

¶¶ I Take Care of My Body

Why? Because my body is the vehicle through which I contact and relate with my world- my husband inclusive- physically and since I have just this one body, it's important that I look after it.

How?

I stay healthy-

Diet: I eat organic food whenever possible, reduce my intake of processed food and pastries, eat lots of fruits and vegetables, take my supplements…

and avoid crash diets. I do indulge myself every now and again, but I tow the line most of the time. I also drink plenty of water.

Exercise: I exercise for at least 30 minutes 3 times a week. (still work in progress 😊). I'm more energetic when I consistently exercise. So, exercising regularly and consistently is always one of my goals.

Sleep and Rest: Besides being good for my mind, rest is great for my body. I look and feel better after I've had time to rest so I take time out to sleep well every night and whenever I feel the need to rest.

Get medical attention:

Besides going for my annual medical check-up, I see a Doctor whenever I have to.

I stay attractive-

I endeavor to keep a neat and well-kept appearance. I pay attention to personal hygiene- take regular baths, brush my teeth, wash my hair. I make my hair, put on some make-up, keep my nails well-manicured. I wear clothes that fit and flatter me. The point is that I do things to add rather than detract from my appeal to my husband. So, I make the effort to look good at home and not only when I have somewhere to go to- occasionally, I might have a lazy day and stay in pajamas for most of the day with my hair wrapped up in a scarf or bonnet, but I'm saying I don't only get dolled up for everyone else to see but my husband. He's important enough to be dressed up for- and while it isn't always the full works I make sure I look nice. Besides making my husband happy, looking good makes me feel good too.

🍴 I Maintain A Healthy Social life

It was never God's intent that I be isolated. God created me to be in community, so I seek godly friendships and support systems. I seek and maintain relationships with people who inspire, encourage, and support me and to whom I can also add value. And importantly, I avoid toxic relationships.

Being socially healthy also means that I cultivate a good reputation. It means I ensure that in all my dealings with people I am honourable- that I am a person of integrity and that I show genuine respect for other people.

¶¶ I Stay Emotionally Healthy

Lastly, I take care of my emotions. I take responsibility for them and manage them.

I understand that while my emotions are important, I'm not to be ruled by them and by having a grip on my emotions, I'm able to positively influence the emotional atmosphere at home.

When my emotions are positive, I use them to infect our home with positive energy! And when they are negative, I reign them in and ensure that I don't say or do something that I'll regret later. Now I'm not saying that I don't express negative emotions, I'm saying that I take control of them and ensure that I express them in ways that don't cause any hurt. So, for example, when I'm angry, I don't try to deal with whatever got me angry until I have taken time to get myself under control- I might walk away, count to ten under my breath or go get a glass of water.

When I honour my husband through the ways I've mentioned- thinking well of him, being faithful, serving him, communicating well, showing him regard and submitting to him. I am showing him that I esteem, love, adore, prize and admire him exceedingly and doing so gives my marriage a higher chance of succeeding.

Okay! Okay! I'm not perfect and I do fail sometimes but here's the point -this is my blueprint for honouring Ossy. So, when and if I fail, I'm quick to repent and get back on track. That's the idea behind this chapter- it's not a source of personal criticism rather a beacon showing me the 'how' and helping me find my way when I get lost.

Chef Tips

✓ Remember, honouring your husband is a choice you make. This choice is not based on whether you think he deserves it. When you honour your husband, you are also honouring God because you are obeying His command.

✓ Pay attention to the messages you've been sending your husband, apologise for any wrong or misunderstood ones.

The Marriage Recipe

Ingredients:

+God
+Love
+Honour

+Lovemaking
+Commitment

Love Making

And the two shall become one flesh'; - Mark 10:8

Just as hot sauce adds a zing to a pot of soup, so sex spices up a marriage. Sex or lovemaking, as I prefer to call it, refers to the physical intimacy between a man and his wife. Don't forget that: it's between a husband and his wife (one man + one woman).

What's so cool about this is that lovemaking is God ordained. From the beginning, lovemaking was an expression of love and intimacy between a husband and wife. It was designed to complement and strengthen the marriage relationship.

When I read Adam's first response to Eve, I see passion; he'd just been presented with this epitome of beauty. He must have been amazed at her shapeliness and beauty... He exclaimed, "This is now bone of my bones and flesh of my flesh" (Gen. 2: 23-24). Scripture goes on to say, "For this reason a man shall leave his father and mother and be joined to his wife, and the two shall become one flesh."(Ephesians 5:31)

One flesh—that's a reference to physical intimacy. The only way two can become one flesh is sexually. God designed the male and female bodies to complement each other that way.

I've learned to always go to the owner's manual to find out how a thing works. It's no different when it comes to lovemaking. Let's see what the Bible has to say about how to make this aspect of marriage beautiful. (This chapter is about lovemaking, so you'll see the word a lot...and I'll use terminology you normally wouldn't use at the dinner table, so please bear with me).

Giving and Receiving Pleasure

Sex is supposed to be pleasurable. It is designed to rouse feelings of satisfaction and enjoyment... like how it feels when I put that first spoonful of my favourite Blue-bunny ice-cream in my mouth after weeks of abstinence. Lovemaking with my husband is even better as there are no disadvantages to a hefty serving and the feelings of satisfaction last for longer. When it comes to sexual pleasure, both my husband and I should experience it. How do I ensure that?

One way is by seeking his pleasure first. Lovemaking is an expression of love, and love does not seek its own. So, when I'm with my husband, I'm thinking about him. How can I please him? How can I satisfy him? How can I make these moments an expression of love? I explore his body; I ask him questions, I learn how he likes to be held, touched. I also make my body available for his enjoyment. I offer it to him as an act of love. I don't deprive him of sexual expression. I let him hold me, touch me, kiss me... And, I take delight in his pleasure. I see my husband as a special treat given to me by God to please and to enjoy! Like my Shulamite sister in the Bible, I engage all our senses in giving and taking pleasure.

Fasten your seatbelt, I'm about to dive in a bit deeper! Using that wonderful Shulamite example from the Song of Solomon, here's how I give and take pleasure...

Touch- referring to everything tactile. Implying everything and anything that brings our bodies in contact with each other. For example, I trace my fingers over Ossy's body- paying attention to the spots and places that give him the most enjoyment. I rub my feet against his, wrap my arms around him, kiss his lips, neck…. I touch him deliberately- to bring him pleasure and because doing so pleases me too. I let him touch me too, making my body his to explore. Now remember I said, I got my cues from the Shulamite? Let's check out her example (all from Song of Solomon)- pay attention to the underlined words (emphasis mine):

"A bundle of myrrh is my beloved to me, That <u>lies all night between my breasts</u>."- 1: 13

"His <u>left hand is under my head</u>, <u>And his right hand embraces me</u>". – 2:6

"Let him kiss me with the kisses of his mouth"— 1:2

Taste- everything to do with flavor and the mouth. Lovemaking involves tasting- the mouth does get involved. Again, let me show you examples from the Song of Solomon;

Like an apple tree among the trees of the woods,
So is my beloved among the sons.
I sat down in his shade with great delight,
<u>And his fruit was sweet to my taste.</u>- 2:3

Your lips, O my spouse,
Drip as the honeycomb;
Honey and milk are under your tongue; -4:11
His mouth is most sweet,
Yes, he is altogether lovely.- 5:16

What's the point of all these examples? To show that sexual pleasure also involves doing stuff that make us taste one another. If that is to be pleasurable then I must taste 'nice' and same goes for Ossy. That means that I tend to my body- I maintain high levels of personal hygiene; regular baths, brush my teeth, use mints, wipes etc. My point? I ensure that when Ossy kisses me, he doesn't have to endure any bad taste. Now since I'm also doing kissing myself, I expect the same standards from my husband. It's a much better experience tasting my husband when his skin and mouth are clean and vice versa.

Smell- pertaining to odour. Everyone (well under normal circumstances) would rather smell something pleasant rather than something foul or unpleasant. With that in mind, I deliberately ensure that I smell good to my husband. When I shop for perfumes, I go for scents my husband likes. Now, don't jump on the women's emancipation train just yet. This isn't about losing self but just practical wisdom. Why would I want to wear a scent that irritates my spouse? I mean even for interviews I know to err on the side of caution with perfumes, so I don't irritate my interviewers and at work, I don't pile up on perfume, so I don't possibly offend my colleagues. Why should I do anything less for my husband? Besides, there're scents I can't stand either- when it comes to perfumes. Some might smell too strong or have undertones that nauseate me. I would consider it inconsiderate if Ossy insisted on wearing one of them – no matter how much he liked them.

Now why did I go off on this perfume trip? Because wearing scents is a great way to enhance or improve the way you smell. But it's not just about putting on some 'Dior or Elizabeth Arden'[27] rather it's about keeping my body smelling attractive. Sometimes all I need to do to achieve that is take a bath and put on some deodorant. Point is, I know that how I smell matters, so I work to keep that smell appealing.

For example, when I've just finished a bout of cooking and as it does most times, the smells from the kitchen have stuck to my clothes and skin, I go take a quick shower before curling up on the sofa with my sweetheart 😊.

And our reference from the Song of Solomon?

How fair is your love, my sister, my spouse! <u>*How much better than wine is your love,*</u>

<u>*And the scent of your perfumes Than all spices!-*</u> *4:10*

Your lips, O my spouse, Drip as the honeycomb; Honey and milk are under your tongue;

<u>*And the fragrance of your garments Is like the fragrance of Lebanon.-*</u> *4:11*

...The fragrance of your breath like apples, - 7:8

While the king is at his table, My spikenard sends forth its fragrance.- 1:12

You get the point. Smelling good is important.

Sight- everything the eyes can see. Looking visually appealing adds enjoyment to our lovemaking. In our bedroom I want to look sexy, provocative, alluring etc. I want to make Ossy desire me with a look, a twirl ... to achieve that, I have to pay attention to the aesthetics of my body. And I'm not talking about being hung up on a perfect body image rather, knowing how to present myself in the most flattering way possible.

No old wrappers tied across the chest or my hair perpetually in a satin bonnet. I only buy and wear lingerie that flatter my figure and appeal to my husband. Remember it's about finding what works for you as a couple. So, strike a balance between what makes you comfortable and what he likes.

Besides lingerie, I also work to keep my body looking good. Thighs getting a little flabby? Time for me to rev up my exercise routine with a focus on lounges and squats. Larger muffin top? Time to cut down on the carbs. My point? It's my responsibility to be able to present my body in the best form I can.

How beautiful are your feet in sandals,
O prince's daughter!
The curves of your thighs are like jewels,
The work of the hands of a skillful workman.

Your navel is a rounded goblet;
It lacks no [a]blended beverage.
Your waist is a heap of wheat
Set about with lilies.

Your two breasts are like two fawns,
Twins of a gazelle.

Your neck is like an ivory tower,
Your eyes like the pools in Heshbon
By the gate of Bath Rabbim.
Your nose is like the tower of Lebanon
Which looks toward Damascus.

Your head crowns you like Mount Carmel,
And the hair of your head is like purple;
A king is held captive by your tresses.

How fair and how pleasant you are,
O love, with your delights!

This stature of yours is like a palm tree,
And your breasts like its clusters.

I know that was a long read, but it's Solomon's account of the beauty that assailed his eyes when he beheld his Shulamite bride. Everything about her was physically attractive- from her hair to her little toes.

That's the idea. Staying attractive, paying attention to my externals so that whenever Ossy sees me he thinks I look lovely.

Sound- all things heard. Can sound add to pleasure during lovemaking? Yes. Why? Because sound can evoke emotions and because sounds can be an expression of satisfaction or pleasure. So how does this help me make our time together more enjoyable? By helping me discover what my husband is enjoying. For example, if I'm giving him a back massage, I can know to keep kneading a spot by paying attention to the sounds he makes. You know just like the way a cat would purr to let you know to keep stroking it? But it's not only the moans of pleasure that enhance lovemaking, but words spoken- the timbre and tone adding flavour too.

Like the Shulamite bride, I say to my husband *'let me hear your voice. For your voice is pleasant'*- Song of Solomon 2:14 and I ensure my voice is pleasant to him too.

No One Size Fits All

When it comes to sexual pleasure, there is no one size fits all description. Why? Because everyone of us is different and unique. That means that how women experience sexual pleasure differs from one woman to the next and even from one sexual encounter to the next.

What's important is finding what fits each individual couple. In my marriage, I work with my husband to make sure we enjoy sex. The key to achieving that lies in discovering what works for us- individually and collectively. And I do that by making my bedroom a place of passionate discovery. I experiment and discover what works and what doesn't work for the both of us. I get to know myself better (and hubby too) and not just my body but my mind and emotions too. For instance, my mood influences my bonding time with hubby, so I work on it. If I feel stressed, before our lovemaking I might take a warm bath with some aromatic bath suds, listen to soft music or maybe spend more time cuddling with my husband. Like I said earlier I pay attention to the things that please my husband and do them. I remain flexible too. What do I mean by that? I mean that just because I've discovered my husband likes to be touched a certain way or in a certain spot, I don't limit myself to touching him only that way. I still try other stuff. Why? Because needs and wants can change and I want to discover them as they do. Both for him and for myself.

Is it possible to increase my experiences of pleasure? Certainly, and the same is true for every woman. How?

- I pay attention to my body, discover what pleases me and let my husband know what I want

- I listen to my husband too, focusing on giving him pleasure the way he wants me to and then I enjoy him enjoying himself.

- I create an atmosphere for lovemaking that appeals to my husband and I – scented sheets, soft music, room the right temperature and snuggled under the covers…Point is, create whatever works for you.

Bottomline, pleasure depends on a willingness to give it, receive it, and share it.

Having a Healthy Sex Life

In order for my sex life to be healthy, my marriage bed must be undefiled. Scripture says:

> *Marriage is to be held in honor among all [that is, regarded as something of great value], and the marriage bed undefiled [by immorality or by any sexual sin]; for God will judge the sexually immoral and adulterous. (Hebrews 13:4 AMPC)*

To defile is to mar or spoil, like climbing unto pristine white sheets with muddied feet. That's what happens when I bring ungodly influences—such as pornography--into our physical intimacy, thus inviting perversion, ungodly expectations, comparisons, and demands into my sex life.

To have a healthy and satisfying sex life, the only experience I need is the one I gain as I make love with my husband. That means that any information gleaned from anywhere else stays outside the door. In other words, rather than looking to contemporary magazines to find out 101 ways to touch my husband, I discover through our lovemaking the 101 ways he likes to be touched☺. It means I don't listen to old wife's tales about what should or shouldn't go on in the bedroom; I look to God's Word, I talk with my hubby, and we discover what we want to allow in the bedroom.

A healthy sex life is one focused on the "now'". It is one that works with the uniqueness of that particular union. It's like a blank canvas with the couple as brushes. Every good artist knows to start off with clean brushes. This keeps the colours true.

A healthy sex life also includes frequent lovemaking. How frequent depends on the couple, but in general and apart from when there are physical limitations, long periods of abstinence should be avoided or at best kept to the minimum.

Now, getting down to the questions you asked in your letter to me. First, Is it a good thing to have sexual relations?

Certainly—but only within a certain context. It's good for a man to have a wife, and for a woman to have a husband. Sexual drives are strong, but marriage is strong enough to contain them and provide for a balanced and fulfilling sexual life in a world of sexual disorder. The marriage bed must be a place of mutuality—the husband seeking to satisfy his wife, the wife seeking to satisfy her husband. Marriage is not a place to "stand up for your rights." Marriage is a decision to serve the other, whether in bed or out. Abstaining from sex is permissible for a period of time if you both agree to it, and if it's for the purposes of prayer and fasting—but only for such times. Then come back together again. Satan has an ingenious way of tempting us when we least expect it. I'm not, understand, commanding these periods of abstinence— only providing my best counsel if you should choose them. (1 Corinthians 7:1-7 Message)

So, I don't withhold sex unless my hubby and I have mutually agreed to abstain for a short while …emphasis on "mutually agreed". I don't "lock the door" even for spiritual reasons (such as times of fasting) unless my husband agrees. I also don't use sex as a bargaining chip, withholding it for favours. That would make me no different from a commercial sex worker, would it not? Nor do I withhold sex as a form of punishment. I don't pay Ossy back for any wrongdoings or misunderstandings by saying no to his advances. Neither do I make excuses to avoid sex. No fictional headaches, feigned exhaustion, fainting spells, and so on. If I don't feel well, that's a different thing. I would say so and expect my husband to understand and let me get better.

Bottomline: I base my expectations about our lovemaking on Scripture, with the goal of loving, pleasing, enjoying and honouring one another so that neither of us is sex- deprived.

Naked and Unashamed

Genesis 2:5 says that before the fall, Adam and his wife were both naked and not ashamed. They were not ashamed of what they looked like and neither shamed the other. That's what God intended and how we should feel about ourselves and our spouses.

My attitude toward my body should be the same as the psalmist's:

> I will give thanks **and** praise to You, for I am **fearfully and wonderfully** made; Wonderful are Your works, **And** my soul knows it very well. (Ps 139:14 AMP)

Knowing that our bodies are *"fearfully and wonderfully made"* is so important. It helps me have a good body image and to appreciate my husband's body too. I see myself as beautiful and my husband as handsome, for God created us wonderfully!

Even though my body looks different from the way it looked when I first got married over a decade ago—I have a few battle scars and the fight against gravity is fiercer!-- when I'm with my husband, I don't see flaws in either of our bodies. I don't make unfavourable comparisons. That model or the movie star with the six-pack? Neither holds a candle to us. My beloved is fearfully and wonderfully made. He is the most handsome of men and all mine to have and enjoy. He can be naked and not ashamed.

Now don't get me wrong; I'm not saying that it's okay to let our bodies go to seed. No way! We both push each other to maintain a healthy lifestyle and to look good. What I'm saying is that I don't compare our stats to anyone else's. We can both be naked and unashamed. I have made my husband's body **the ideal,** and that makes our times behind closed doors so beautiful. I'm constantly reminded of how blessed I am to have such awesome workmanship to enjoy!

The key thought is this: I don't allow comparisons or criticisms in our marriage bed. Not even in my thoughts. What I have is the best there is for me!

Sexual Problems

Just like in every other area of life, it is possible to have problems in one's sex life. While this list is not exhaustive, I want to briefly talk about a couple of issues that can cause one or both people to be frustrated or unhappy sexually.

Frigidity or impotence. If you are frigid or your husband is impotent, I urge you to seek professional help as the cause could be medical or psychological. In addition to getting professional help, I encourage you to find scriptures that show you that it's God's will you have a fulfilling sex life and make daily, personalized confessions of those verses. (Song of Solomon is a good place to start). To those confessions add scriptures on health and healing. Like, Exodus 15:26 - *For I am the Lord who heals you.* God has made provision for us to be healed – in every way. And remember to face this together as a couple, supporting each other.

Lack of chemistry. I think this is one of the easiest sexual problems to deal with. Why? Because chemistry is something you can create. Chemistry is science, like how hydrogen +oxygen = water. If I want to create water, I must bring those two elements together.

What is involved in creating sexual chemistry with your hubby?

Attraction (Sensual Input) + Similarities (Agreement) + Communication (Listen + Share) + Sincerity (No Hidden Agenda) = CHEMISTRY

Want to create chemistry with your spouse? Ensure the sensory input during lovemaking is pleasant. Look good, smell nice, taste nice. Focus more on the things you can agree on. It's easier to be attracted to someone you're not constantly fighting with. Communicate with each other; talk kindly. Most importantly, listen to what you are both saying and finally show each other that you can be trusted.

In this chapter I've been exploring how having a vibrant love life enhances my marriage. How by committing to work with my husband on this aspect of my marriage, I add value to our relationship. In the words of Solomon's Shulamite bride;

'I am my beloved's, And my beloved is mine.'- Song of Solomon 6:3.

That's what love making is all about- me for my husband and my husband for me. But before I leave this, I would like to add- the greatest source for romantic, custom geared, expert ideas, solutions, repair kits for any problems in the bedroom is the Holy Spirit. Remember, He is the greatest teacher- if there's anything you don't know or need help with… ask Him.

Chef Tips

✓ Next time you make love, spend some time exploring and discovering the man God gave you. Get to know what makes him tick.

✓ Learn what gives you sexual pleasure and share what you discover with your husband.

✓ Schedule a romantic date and pull out all the stops. Invest in some new lingerie, put perfume on your sheets, buy some scented candles or aromatic oils, give each other a massage, play some love songs and slow dance to them... let the Holy Spirit inspire you.

The Marriage Recipe

Ingredients:

+ God
+Love
+Honour
+Lovemaking

+Commitment

Commitment

"Don't ask me to leave you and turn back. Wherever you go,
I will go; wherever you live, I will live. Your people will be
my people, and your God will be my God. Wherever you die,
I will die, and there I will be buried. - Ruth 1:16 (NLT)

The last ingredient in this marriage recipe is commitment. I liken commitment to adding leavening to my recipe. A leavening agent produces an altering or transforming influence [28]. An example is yeast, there's a lot that can be said about the chemistry of yeast in food, but what interests me with respect to this analogy is the tenacity of yeast- its role is to break up whatever resistance sugar or carbohydrates present in the recipe and cause the dough to rise.

In my marriage, I need that kind of stubbornness. I need commitment. According to the dictionary, *commitment is* a promise or firm decision to do or give something.

So, commitment is not just a word or words, but actions; it's a decision. It's me making up my mind to make my marriage work. Until I do, that picture of a marriage paradise I painted at the beginning will remain nothing but beautiful picture in my mind.

In a sense, commitment is the ingredient that wraps up all the other elements of the recipe. Much like how a tortilla wrap keeps all the other pieces in a tortilla in place. All the other ingredients must go hand in hand with commitment otherwise they won't work.

If I don't make the decision and follow through with it to do all the things I've mentioned I need to do to keep my marriage successful- get God involved, love and honour my husband, have a healthy sex life- then my marriage recipe will fall to pieces.

Commitment is a no turning back and a living up to all my promises to my husband and God kind of attitude. Commitment means that I have decided to do all that is dependent on me to make my marriage work; I will do all that is in my power to succeed at my marriage. It means that I don't mind the hard work.

A good example of commitment can be found in the story of Ruth and Naomi and although this is an example of a different kind of relationship (one between daughter in-law and mother-in- law) the same principles apply. And from the book of Ruth I draw the following characteristics, commitment;

- is a deliberate choice I must make for myself.

No one other than I can make the decision to be committed. I cannot depend on external motivators to keep me in my marriage. You know that saying *'you can lead a horse to the water, but you can't make it drink?'*[29] Nobody can make me want to have a happy marriage, I must want to stay married and be willing to do what it takes to make a happy home.

- involves my willingness to stand by my husband in the good and bad times.

Traditional wedding vows include the clause 'for better or worse and in sickness and in health'. Why is that? Because life can sometimes throw us bad times too. Truth is, there's no guarantee that any one of us will have a problem free life. Not even as a Christian. What we're promised as followers of Christ is that He will never leave us nor forsake us, no matter what! (Hebrews 13:5) That is an example or promise of God being committed to His children. For my marriage to work, I must have that kind of attitude. I am willing to stand by Ossy not only when everything is rosy- healthy finances, physical health etc. but also when we face the down times. Just like Ruth did with Naomi, I do everything possible to help us back up on our feet when we are down, without feeling frustrated and without throwing everything I do to help in my husband's face.

I've seen marriages go into crisis because the man of the house lost his job or means of livelihood. Suddenly because the wife had to bring in all the funds she becomes frustrated and makes her husband feel less than a man. That's so wrong! In a situation like that, what am I expected to do? Everything I can to help with the finances- work 9-5, find creative ways to earn extra income (provide private catering, join a network marketing company etc.) and most importantly provide encouragement to my husband so he can find his way back on his feet. My husband is not the head of our home just because he can provide for us, he's the head because God made him that! And God gave me to my husband, so Ossy would have a helping hand. So, when I help Ossy, I've done nothing out of the ordinary, it's my responsibility. And the fact that I help doesn't subtract from my husband's role or position in our home.

That's the attitude Ruth had, she didn't think it was beneath her to go glean in the fields so she could bring food back for Naomi and herself. She would do that and still come home and show the utmost respect to her mother-in-law- she was committed to Naomi. That's what I mean, I am committed to Ossy in the same way.

- involves work, sometimes hard work.

Working in those fields must have been hard work for Ruth. But she kept going back. Why? For Naomi's sake. That's commitment. In the same way, there're times when I am inconvenienced or stretched so I can provide support to my husband or so that I can be the kind of wife God expects me to be. For instance, when I take a night job, so I can still help with the finances while reducing the cost of child-care-that's commitment. When I reign in my temper, so I don't say the wrong things when Ossy and I have misunderstandings- that's commitment. My point? Sometimes, being the kind of wife God expects me to be is hard. But commitment keeps me doing what's right and what's needed.

- involves patience

I talked about patience when I talked about prayer and love but that's not the only areas I need patience for. Creating a good marriage takes time. That's where patience comes in. I must stay in the process, that takes commitment. I don't give up. I wake up each morning ready to do my bit to ensure that my marriage is healthy.

When I got married, I said the traditional vows;

"I, Mfon, take you, Ossy, for my lawful husband, to have and to hold from this day forward, for better, for worse, for richer, for poorer, in sickness and in health, until death do us part. I will love and honor you all the days of my life."

Being committed to my marriage means that I keep these vows. Over the years, in addition to those first vows, my internal conviction about my marriage sounds somewhat like this-

"I, Mfon, take you, Ossy, to be my wedded husband. With deepest joy I come into my new life with you. As you have pledged to me your life and love, so I too happily give you my life, and in confidence submit myself to your headship as to the Lord. As is the church in her relationship to Christ, so I will be to you Ossy, I will live first unto our God and then unto you, loving you, obeying you, caring for you and ever seeking to please you. God has prepared me for you and so I will ever strengthen, help, comfort, and encourage you. Therefore, throughout life, no matter what may be ahead of us, I pledge to you my life as an obedient and faithful wife."[30]

It's my responsibility to stay true to these promises and as I do that, I'm continually creating a successful marriage.

Chef Tips

✓ Make a commitment to God and your husband to be the kind of wife God wants you to be. Start by revisiting your marriage vows.

Conclusion

You can have a successful marriage

Like I learnt many years ago, marriage can be either a prison or paradise. Creating either scenario is dependent on two factors- the husband and the wife. There can be no successful marriage without the input of the two.

In this book, I have shown you how as a wife I'm doing my bit to contribute to the success of my marriage. How I am using practical tips from the Bible to make my home a haven. This marriage recipe is in no way exhaustive, but I have covered the basic ingredients needed to make a marriage thrive. Every other thing that could contribute to a successful marriage builds on these five ingredients- God, love, honour, lovemaking and commitment. I believe that the principles I've shared here would work for anyone given the right circumstances.

Again, marriage takes two, but I've focused here on one half- the wife. So here I've made little mention of what a husband should do to make his marriage work. It doesn't mean that he doesn't have a role to play in creating the dream marriage.

But here's the thing, if each partner is the spouse God intended then there's a higher chance of their marriage thriving. So as a wife, because I stick to the Biblical blueprint for marriage, I am creating the marriage of my dreams.

I close this chapter with a focus on the word, 'blueprint'. That's what the book is, a blue print for married life. It's not an instrument of criticism, rather it's to show God's standard for a wife. As we often do, I fail every now and then but looking into God's word, I can see where I need to make adjustments or corrections when I do.

My prayer is that as you go through this book, you find encouragement to look at your life and make the necessary adjustments needed to fit God's standard for a wife and thus create your own marriage paradise.

References

1 English-Oxford Living Dictionaries
2 English-Oxford Living Dictionaries
3 English-Oxford Living Dictionaries
4 Greek word for Helper
5 English-Oxford Living Dictionaries
6 TV series
7 www.dictionary.com
8 Baker's Evangelical Dictionary of Biblical Theology
9 www.dictionary.com
10 Covenant Christian Centre- In a NUTSHELL, September 2, 2018
11 local Nigerian ingredients
12 Merriam- Webster Dictionary
13 STRONGS NT 5281: ὑπομονή
14 Google dictionary
15 "If you say that someone has lost the battle, but won the war, you mean that although they have been defeated in a small conflict they have won a larger, more important one of which it was a part" – Collins English Dictionary
16 Google dictionary
17 Dictionary of Bible Themes 5813
18 Google dictionary
19 Strong's Concordance).
20 Thesaurus.com
21 Oxford Living Dictionaries
22 Wikipedia
23 Merriam-Webster Dictionary
24 TV Character from NCIS
25 Cambridge English Dictionary
26 Merriam- Webster Dictionary
27 Designer perfume brand names
28 www.dictionary.com

29 "You can give someone an advantage or provide them with an opportunity, but you can't force them to do something if they don't want to."- Farlex Dictionary of Idioms. © 2015 Farlex, Inc, all rights reserved

30 Sample wedding vow taken from- https://bible.org/article/sample-wedding-vows

Printed in the United States
By Bookmasters